Giving Good Feedback

Giving Good Feedback

Margaret Cheng

GIVING GOOD FEEDBACK

Published with permission from *The Economist* by Pegasus Books.

The Economist is an imprint of
Pegasus Books, Ltd.
148 West 37th Street, 13th Floor
New York, NY 10018

ISBN: 978-1-63936-479-4

10 9 8 7 6 5 4 3 2 1

Printed in the United States of America
Distributed by Simon & Schuster
www.pegasusbooks.com

PEGASUS BOOKS
NEW YORK LONDON

For Steve

About the author

Margaret Cheng has 30 years' experience as a senior HR manager, executive, career coach and consultant, and director of a social enterprise. She has worked in a range of sectors, from retail and financial services through to consultancies and charities. She writes on business-related topics for HR, outplacement and career coaching consultancies and *CIPD* magazine and has appeared on *Working Lunch*. Margaret has also been published by *26*, Bloomsbury Festival and *Friends on the Shelf* and has read and performed on Bloomsbury Radio and at the Foundling Museum.

Contents

Introduction: The Four Horsemen of the Apocalypse

A long time ago, in the testosterone-fuelled world that was the financial services sector in the 1990s, four very senior managers found their way to the HR department.

Like the Four Horsemen of the Apocalypse, they came with doom-laden messages.

"I need you to have a word with Bill. People are leaving in droves because of him."

"You have to talk to Reuben. No one will sit next to him."

"You've got to sort Belinda out before I strangle her."

"Look what Phil's done now. I don't believe he's still doing this."

It seemed that Bill walked around with his head in the air, yelling things at staff like, "That wasn't a request, Clive, just do it!"; Belinda kept shredding important documents by mistake; and Phil had sent an email to a new member of staff with the subject heading "Yet another stupid thing you've done in the space of half an hour you complete ****wit".

Reuben was the most straightforward of the four issues. Nobody wanted to sit next to him because he had a body odour problem.

The four horsemen were very senior, otherwise capable managers. None of them had tried talking to their staff about the impact of their behaviours on the organisation or the people around them. They did not know how, and they did not want to learn. They were hoping HR could just sort it out for them, so they did not have to give *feedback*.

It turned out that the horsemen really were heralding an apocalypse. Not long afterwards, the firm collapsed dramatically, in the wake of a high-profile financial scandal.

I always wondered if the inability to give feedback was a significant contributory factor in the collapse. There were certainly quite a few Belindas at work, shredding important documents without understanding the consequences.

Of course, the four horsemen were not alone. Many people find giving feedback difficult and would rather leave it to others or hope the person concerned works it out for themselves.

And since the time of the four horsemen, the whole landscape around interpersonal relationships at work has been transformed. In the modern workplace, giving and receiving feedback at work is more important than ever as collaboration rather than top-down command-and-control leadership has become the order of the day. That doesn't make it any easier; it can feel more fraught and more complex than ever.

But difficult though you may find it, giving, receiving and soliciting feedback is critical to your development and growth as a human being – let alone as a leader. Most people want to do a good job at work, but it's not always easy to know how to improve and grow. Feedback is about *learning*: you cannot learn, or help others to learn, without it.

This book is divided into three parts and is designed to take you on a journey. At the beginning of each section, there are some questions for you to think about, so that you can link your own experience to the topics covered as you read.

By the time you have finished reading, you will have the answers to three key questions.

- Why is feedback so important?
- Why is it so hard?
- What can I do to make it easier?

Part 1 looks at what feedback is and explains why it is so important to do it well.

In basic terms, feedback is about communication. In a simple communication loop, it's what closes that loop so that you know your message has been received and (you hope) understood. At work, it's a crucial tool for helping people to understand their impact and supporting their development.

However, feedback has been the subject of much recent thinking and debate.

At one end of the spectrum, the Silicon Valley experiments in radical transparency champion cultures where robust, frequent, candid and often critical feedback are seen as the way forward. Alternatively, Marcus Buckingham and Ashley Goodall's feedback fallacy explores the limits of feedback, suggesting why it's not the route to improvement that we might think it is.

In the light of these debates, Part 1 explores how things can go wrong, both in the way people give feedback and the way they receive it and what makes it helpful or unhelpful. I take the idea of the feedback fallacy and turn this round to show that this is exactly why giving good feedback is hard but essential.

I also introduce my **giving good feedback framework**, which links the idea of a communication loop with David Kolb's experiential learning circle. Forward-looking constructive feedback helps people move around the learning circle, via the key steps of experience, reflection and practice.

Part 2 explores the idea that to give feedback well, you must start with yourself.

Everyone, consciously or not, has experiences and biases that can get in the way of giving good feedback. The trick is to improve your awareness of them so that you can work to overcome and mitigate them – and also understand how people on the receiving end might be feeling.

You'll be asked to consider what influences these areas have had on your own approach and responses to giving and receiving feedback, as well as your openness to asking for feedback on your own performance and behaviours.

And because no one works in isolation, I also explore how your approach to feedback is affected by organisational culture and consider how psychological safety can support positive feedback cultures.

There is a distinction between organisation-wide performance management systems and good, regular developmental feedback as part of everyday conversations and communication.

As part of those everyday conversations, I also look at the importance of clear expectations in supporting good feedback at work.

Part 3 pulls everything together to offer support via a range of practical models and tools to make giving good feedback a routine part of your relationships at work.

It provides feedback and communication models, runs through practical examples, and invites you to work through checklists and case studies using your own examples.

You'll be reminded of the purpose of good feedback and the giving good feedback framework, starting with a clear assessment of what you want to give feedback on. There'll be guidance on how to articulate this in terms of clear, behaviour-related examples and advice in planning the conversations to get this across.

I also look at the emotions that people might experience when receiving feedback and guide you through planning and preparing for the more difficult conversations. I include empathy-mapping models and ways of handling reactions, for when feedback does not land as we intend.

Whatever you think about feedback, it remains an essential part of all communications and relationships – at work and elsewhere. Whether you love it, hate it, embrace it or avoid it, it's simply a fact of life. What follows offers a route map and guide to its power and pitfalls. The aim is to support you to feel much more equipped to give good feedback – at work, at home and anywhere else you choose.

PART 1

What is feedback and why does it matter?

This section acts as an introduction to the concept of feedback, offering an easy-to-read digest of popular models, beliefs and opinions about feedback.

First, though, consider what the term "feedback" means to you. Grab a pen and a bit of paper, ready to make a few notes. Then have a think about it in these two situations.

1. Your personal experience of receiving feedback (from school, parents, friends, even enemies)
   What examples do you have? Can you remember the earliest piece of feedback you received?

2. Your experience of receiving feedback at work
   What different experiences of feedback have you had at different jobs? Any inspirational supportive feedback or truly awful comments that were intended to be helpful? What organisational feedback systems have you had to navigate? What impact have they had on you and your team?

Then, as you start reading, you will be able to compare my definition of feedback with the way you have experienced feedback in your home life and in your working life. You can then explore the theory behind feedback, consider the power it has and understand why it matters to do it well.

Practical stories and examples will help you reflect on your own experience and make sense of the theory.

The section also introduces my model for giving good feedback. This will provide:

- a process for you to gather your thoughts when considering feedback conversations
- an easy way of structuring feedback, linked to observable behaviours.

Used properly, this model will also act as an antidote to any complications you may experience when trying to give good feedback at work.

Are you ready? Then we'll begin. It starts with a story.

Of course it does. Everything to do with feedback starts with a story.

1

What is feedback?

"Feedback is the breakfast of champions."

Ken Blanchard[1]

After scooting down the hill from his villa in Spain to his shared workspace on the beach, Mike Jones glanced at the flyer offering remote coaching sessions on how to give good feedback.

He was glad to have left the corporate rat race so that he didn't have to bother about things like how to give good feedback anymore. After years working in banks, he and a childhood friend, Elliot, had decided to set up their own business, providing data to guide banks on their environmental, social and governance obligations. They believed in the value of their product and were doing well. Life was good.

Then Elliot (on Zoom) said something about Mike being slow with a marketing spec. He followed this up with something that Mike thought didn't sound like Elliot at all. "I want to be honest and candid with you, Mike. This has had an impact. Sales figures are down."

Suddenly life didn't feel quite so good. The words "honest" and "candid" always meant trouble, in Mike's experience. He sat up straighter and swallowed. "Hang on, a minute," he said. "Is that feedback?"

He grabbed a notebook and pen and looked expectantly at the camera.

Elliot fiddled with his own pen for a minute. Then he said, "No, mate, I'm just saying sales have dropped fifty per cent."

"Oh, right," said Mike, putting his pen down and relaxing again. No feedback. It was OK.

It took him a few minutes to recover from the shock of potentially having been given feedback by his partner. Then he thought: did Elliot say something about sales being fifty per cent down? How come?

No escape from feedback

Even without the impetus of poor sales, the pressure to give feedback seems as impossible to outrun as the original Four Horsemen of the Apocalypse.

On a recent morning, I was asked to rate my experience of a hotel website, comment on my ticket-buying experience with a train company, fill in a questionnaire about a medical service and give stars to a couple of purchases on Amazon that I have no memory of making. I also spent an anxious hour reviewing social media posts about a new creative project, worried about the number of likes and was distracted by comments on my work from people I have never met and have no interest in.

I imagine that, like me, you get bombarded with requests for feedback after making even minimal use of any kind of service or product. If not today, at least some time this week.

Then there is always the risk of receiving an avalanche of feedback in return. Feedback on your feedback, in other words.

LinkedIn, for example, offers me a weekly feedback summary detailing the number of comments and likes on my posts, ending with a tantalising comment, something like "and your profile has been viewed four times this week, Margaret! Click here to find out more about your viewers." Tantalising, because finding out more involves not just clicking but also paying more and installing some extra feature.

Happily, I can avoid this particular feedback; all I have to do is not pay. It is not as easy to avoid elsewhere. Like it or not, it seems that feedback plays a critical role everywhere in our world, both personally and professionally.

You might therefore conclude that I could make a leap of faith and assume that you now know all there is to know about what feedback looks like. So starting with a chapter headed "What is feedback?" might seem strange.

But carry out any kind of survey – a Google search, a review of academic literature, or even mention that you are writing a book about feedback to your friends – and you will find that the word "feedback" prompts an enormous range of comments and experiences. These often go on for a long time, detailing varied, complex (and, on occasion, frankly traumatic) feedback experiences and quandaries.

As a result, before I start looking in detail at how to give good feedback at work, I feel I should alert you to one of the sacred tenets of feedback. This is that good feedback involves good communication. And just because the term "feedback" is a big part of our world, this does not mean that:

- we all have the same understanding and expectations of that activity, or
- that we feel comfortable about doing it, or

- that we all do it in the same way.

So, in the spirit of modelling good communication skills, when I use the term "feedback", let me first explain what I mean.

What is feedback?

If you look through a dictionary you will find several definitions for "feedback", with example sentences showing how you can use the word. Some are more helpful than others. The online *Cambridge Dictionary* includes:

> "Jimi Hendrix loved to fling his guitar around to get weird and wonderful sounds from the feedback."

> "Feedback from the sensors ensures that the car engine runs smoothly."

> "Have you had any feedback from the customers about the new soap?"

And then we have the following definition taken from Google's English dictionary (provided by Oxford Languages):

> **feedback** *noun* (opinion) Information about reactions to a product, a person's performance of a task, etc. which is used as a basis for improvement.

If you like to make notes as you read, you might want to write down the three points, next to this last definition of feedback. These are:

- information
- opinion
- reactions.

These are all critical for you to bear in mind as you explore more about what the term "feedback" actually means.

Giving feedback is a basic human skill, based on the ability to communicate. When you give feedback, you are simply communicating information, your opinion about and reactions to something someone has done. Elliot, for example, was trying to communicate his view that Mike's slow production of the marketing spec had had a direct impact on sales.

As humans, we are social creatures. We are always communicating, whether we do it consciously or not. So giving and receiving feedback is something we do all the time, whether we are aware of it or not.

The key message of this book is:

Feedback is always about communication. In a simple communication loop, it's the thing that closes that loop so that you know your message has been received and (hopefully) understood.

It starts right at the beginning, when you are trying to acquire all the skills you need to get through life.

Learning through communication

To acquire any life skills, you have to be able to learn.

Take motor skills – walking, for example. As a child, you learn to walk by trying it out, falling over and trying again. If you are lucky, your learning is enhanced by having friendly adults around to encourage you as you develop this basic skill.

"Three more steps! Keep going! Well done."

The same friendly adults might then go on to give you more

detailed feedback about the impact of more nuanced behaviour, such as the tantrum you have later.

"Screaming hurts my ears! Use your words!"

Once you can "use your words", you learn that it is more efficient to ask for what you want instead of just pointing and yelling. It's better to explain how you feel, rather than stamp and scream.

You have learnt this social construct largely because of the feedback communicated to you from those around you. This process continues as you grow up.

Learning through feedback

There are many different theories about how we learn. David Kolb's experiential learning theory helps explain the link between feedback and learning in more detail.

Kolb described the process for good learning in the following steps.[2]

1. **The learner has a concrete experience** (a new experience or a reinterpretation of an existing experience).

- In our tantrum example, this is when an adult puts their hands over their ears and says, "Stop screaming, use your words."

- In Elliot and Mike's example, the fall in sales means they need to do something differently. Elliot tries giving Mike feedback about his contribution to this situation.

2. **The learner reflects and observes the new experience** (any inconsistencies between experience and understanding are particularly important).

- You might think about the adult's reaction to your tantrum and wonder about the difference between this and their reaction to when you smile and wave at them in the supermarket.
- Mike wonders about the drop in sales and why Elliot is talking to him like that.

3. **The learner has new ideas as a result** (abstract conceptualisation, where reflection gives rise to the new idea or modification to an existing abstract concept).

- You think about new ways to get what you want instead of using your previous approach of screaming.
- Mike realises that Elliot is trying to give him feedback. For the first time he and Elliot consider that they need to learn different ways to communicate to keep their business going.

4. **The learner actively experiments** (applying these ideas to the world about them to see the results).

- You try using your words, by saying, "Please may I have that biscuit?" You find that this results in your mother smiling and giving you a biscuit. You decide to try this approach again in future.
- Mike and Elliot practise different ways of communicating. Once they are able to offer each other feedback (following their "giving good feedback" coaching), their sales start to improve.

And so you learn to develop your use of words, your communication skills, even if this is initially only to get what you want in life. This early form of feedback closes the loop for you, in the same way that falling over does when you start to walk. And this learning continues throughout your life, as you build personal and business relationships and learn new skills.

For example, learning the skills required to develop and grow a business. In their new role as business owners, Elliot and Mike's long history has acted as both a hindrance and a help. They are comfortable with each other but are not used to challenging each other or asking too many questions. As business partners, they have to learn to communicate in a different way. This means giving each other feedback about the impact their behaviours have, both on each other and on the work they need to do for their business. Their sales will not improve until they have learnt to give each other good feedback.

Kolb developed his ideas into an experiential learning cycle, shown in Figure 1.

As you go through life and learn from many diverse experiences, you will move around this experiential cycle again and again, trying a different strategy for each situation.

Feedback at work

Once you have made it into the world of work, the reward on offer for any accomplishments will be a salary instead of biscuits. But to continue learning, you will still need other people to tell you the impact that you and your behaviour have on them and on the work you are doing together.

If you are lucky, the feedback you get at work will be helpful and supportive, encouraging you round this experiential learning cycle. If you are unfortunate, you will encounter at least one of the Four Horsemen of the Apocalypse, together with all their limitations.

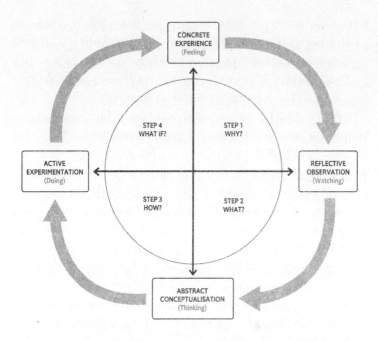

Figure 1. David Kolb's experiential learning cycle[3]

But therapeutic though it might be for me to tut at their feedback reluctance, the four horsemen are not that unusual. If you are completely honest with yourself, might you be perfectly happy to put two stars on an Amazon review to rate a disappointing purchase? Then, when asked for feedback in your workplace, you find you share the same feelings as our four horsemen? That is, you would prefer to put off giving (and receiving) feedback at work for ever?

You are not alone. Many people are the opposite of comfortable in giving feedback; many otherwise capable people panic when they are required to give feedback in person in the world of work. Part of the reason is because feedback is so often an organisational requirement, headed by a specialist department such as human resources or talent management and labelled with a great big capital F. That capital F stands for a prescribed activity: Giving Feedback at Work.

This specialist department will probably run helpful training sessions, explaining that Giving Feedback at Work is an important part of your role. When Giving Feedback at Work, you must be objective, there are competency frameworks to refer to, job descriptions and ranking information to consult.[4] You might also be required to link your feedback with ratings, 360 processes[5] and appraisal processes.[6]

And now, as Mike succinctly put it, referring to his corporate life before Spain, the great big capital F in Giving Feedback at Work just stands for great big fat Fail.

This is because, whatever the limitations of these processes, you will be forced to use them. Your team members will probably want to argue about your decision to rate them with 3 instead of 4, or see themselves as worthy of being described as an over-achiever rather than an under-achiever. They may also ask for your comments about their possible progress to a promotion, or insist they want to be told where they stand.

A senior manager once told me she had booked herself onto a two-week conference in Washington simply because the title of one half-hour talk appealed. It was called "Ouch! That hurt! The neurobiology of feedback!" At the time, the organisation was developing its 360-degree feedback process and the experience had been painful for all concerned.

None of this has anything to do with helpful feedback, of course. It is also quite a lot to handle, on top of your day job.

Carrying the weight of all these Giving Feedback at Work expectations, many people shy away from giving feedback at all, feeling it is best to play it safe and say as little as possible, as blandly as possible. Or like the four horsemen, just pass this whole Giving Feedback at Work business back to the human resources or talent management department. After all, it was their idea in the first place.

However, it does not have to be like this. Let's go back to our original question.

What is feedback #2?

All these systems, appraisals, competency frameworks, ratings and missives from human resources departments are red herrings when trying to understand what feedback is.

Remember: giving feedback is a natural human activity, something we all do as part of our communication with each other. By the time you start work and become confused by organisational labelling, you will have received many kinds of feedback.

What did you note down when thinking about your personal experiences of feedback before starting to read this chapter? I imagine most of those feedback experiences did not come with a big label, signalling Feedback. You may just have had a warm glow when a parent noticed and appreciated something you did, a sense of unfairness if a teacher criticised you for something you did not do, or felt demotivated by a disappointing test result that did not reward you for your hard work.

Now you are grown up, a simple communication loop with your life partner or flatmate may involve communicating how you feel about a particular behaviour (for example, cooking a lovely meal, helping or not helping to clear up), the impact of this on you (for example, it makes you feel appreciated/looked after/annoyed), and what you would like to happen instead (for example, share tasks or take turns).

As you build your relationship, practise your communication skills and learn to navigate your way round the barriers, you will each begin to notice the times when the other is more receptive, the sort of comments they respond to, the sort of tasks they enjoy and the ones they need more support with. You will both adapt your communication accordingly. At this point, you are both learning to give good feedback.

You are, however, unlikely to sit down with each other and develop a complex system, detailing the standards of vacuuming and menu choices expected, in order to facilitate an annual evaluation of your individual contributions to the cleaning or cooking activities of the household.

The reality is that no one improves their feedback-giving skills by focusing on systems and processes. In fact, if you try, you will end up giving feedback that can be at best unhelpful and at worst actively damaging. Once a natural human activity has been labelled with a capital letter and turned into a system, it can seem impossibly complex.

This is unfortunate. Your need for feedback at work is just as critical to your development and growth as your need for feedback at home. At work, feedback remains a crucial tool for helping people understand their impact on others and supporting their development. Forward-looking constructive feedback helps you and your team learn and move round the learning circle described by Kolb, via the key steps of experience, observation, reflection and practice.

So, for example, when a meeting goes well or goes completely off track, feedback is the way you communicate to your colleague:

- what you saw them doing (for example, talking over the client, when they tried to make a point)
- the impact these actions had on you
- the impact you think these actions had on other people
- the resulting impact you think these actions had on the outcome of the meeting.

In theory, this should mean that giving feedback is straightforward. In practice, of course, no one finds it easy.

For this reason, as well as offering courses on giving feedback, many companies offer communication skills courses. These can be extremely helpful. However, in linking communication to feedback at work, there are two models of communication that are useful to consider. One is from the ancient Greek philosopher Aristotle[7] and the other is from communications theorist David Berlo.[8]

Aristotle's model puts the speaker at the centre of any communication, responsible for the result and the impact on the audience. Most organisations that are trying to support their managers to improve their feedback-giving skills follow Aristotle's communication model.

All the emphasis for the success of the feedback message is placed on the speaker (i.e. the feedback giver) rather than the audience (i.e. the person receiving the feedback). As a result, training at work will generally focus on offering the feedback giver a variety of feedback giving tips and techniques to adapt the message for the occasion, to achieve maximum effect with the audience. If we have a difficult piece of feedback to impart, we spend a lot of time planning our message, hoping that the person we are giving feedback to will get the point.

This is, of course, important; the feedback we give will have an impact.

But good feedback is not just a matter of *what* that feedback is about; it also needs to focus on *how* it is given: that is, not just focusing on the message, but also on the way we talk to the person, how we react and adapt our communication as the discussion progresses.

Berlo pays more attention to the state of the receiver when completing a communication loop. In terms of feedback, you may have all the right elements to put together the message – you can be very well prepared, have gathered perfect examples, expressed yourself clearly, respectfully and helpfully, used exactly the right sort of language. Yet still the message may not land correctly. In this case, you need to think a bit more about the channel and the receiver.

The key message here is that **feedback is as much about the person receiving the message as it is about the person giving it**. There can be a whole range of reasons why the person may not be able to receive that feedback well. These are just as important to consider as developing your own skills and techniques.

The closing of a communication loop generally involves putting yourself in the other person's shoes. This is something we might understand in other types of communication, but when giving one-to-one feedback at work, it's often forgotten. So, thinking back to the definition of feedback (on page 14), it is important to remember that feedback will always involve two people.

Feedback at work #2

One of the reasons we forget this simple message is that there can be other peculiar things going on in the work environment. For example, providing or processing feedback remotely can make this natural process feel a little strange. As remote working has increased and global management roles become the norm in many industries, there has been a corresponding rise in the number of people who find it hard to process feedback remotely.

An Australian client of mine, Andy, called, reeling with shock. He had been summoned to a Zoom meeting at the end of his working day and threatened with dismissal. Brian, his manager, told him his contract would be closed "due to ongoing poor attitude" unless he changed his ways immediately.

"What poor attitude?" Andy wanted to know.

"The one you have consistently had feedback about for the last two years," said Brian.

Andy had no idea what he was talking about. He had had a few Zoom chats with Brian, sure, good conversations he thought, shooting the breeze. How was he supposed to know he was being given feedback? It didn't come with a label.

Andy listened to Brian in disbelief. He was thinking, "It's not like you know anything about my actual job or my day-to-day work. You are only the manager because you suck up to the managing director. I keep the Australian office going. I know what needs doing, what works, what doesn't. What would you be giving me feedback about exactly? Who do you think you are? My boss?"

Then Brian took him by surprise, saying frostily, "None of us likes working with someone with your attitude – the one you're demonstrating at the moment, in the disrespectful way you just spoke to me."

Too late, Andy realised he had spoken his thoughts out loud. (He tells me he always says what he thinks. He thought Brian and his other colleagues liked it. He's pretty sure none of them have ever told him they don't. Or if they did, Andy thought they were joking and didn't take them seriously.)

What should he do now, Andy wanted to know. How was he supposed to learn a different attitude at his age? It was easy for Brian to say it was disrespectful. What did that mean, anyway?

Unknown to Andy, however, Brian was also calling me for help. He was a relatively new manager, with a lot of responsibilities. On the same day that he spoke to Andy, he also had to tell an experienced team leader in Cape Town, via a flickering screen, that he wasn't meeting his targets, give a young consultant in Sydney feedback on her selling skills, and articulate to a recently promoted assistant in Delhi what their likely progress through the company would be.

He was painfully aware that they all expected different things from him when they asked for feedback. He knew some members of his team were looking for him to help them build self-esteem or gain empowerment. Others expected ideas on how they could build on what they thought they had already done brilliantly. Then there was Andy, to whom feedback seemed to be the equivalent of water off a duck's back – it just seemed to roll off him, without making so much as a dent in his enormous ego.

Brian quite reasonably wondered how on earth he was supposed to give feedback in this strange new world where there were already so many complications, let alone how he might translate any of it into good feedback.

Brian put off the conversation with Andy about his attitude because he found it uncomfortable to talk to someone who seemed so confident, and he found it even harder over Zoom. Elliot put off his conversation with Mike because he didn't want to upset his friend by suggesting that their poor sales were down to him.

We will talk about this more in later chapters. However, both men were doing their colleagues a disservice. Feedback for their colleagues would have been helpful. They just weren't quite sure where to start. And, as we have already explored, once a natural human activity has been labelled and treated as a corporate process, it can seem much more complex. Even more so if it is delivered via a computer screen.

But the good news for Brian, Elliot and for you is that it is possible to keep the process of giving (and receiving) feedback at work both simple and useful. All you need to do is to rethink how you plan, deliver and question it. The giving good feedback framework, with no capital letters, is here to help.

The giving good feedback framework

Figure 2 shows what giving good feedback should be about.[9] The focus is on observed behaviours and the aim is to help people work round the four stages of Kolb's learning circle.

When you get confused by the whole process, remember that these rating and appraisal systems are not important. What is important is being able to give and receive *good feedback*.

That is, you need to be able to communicate what you

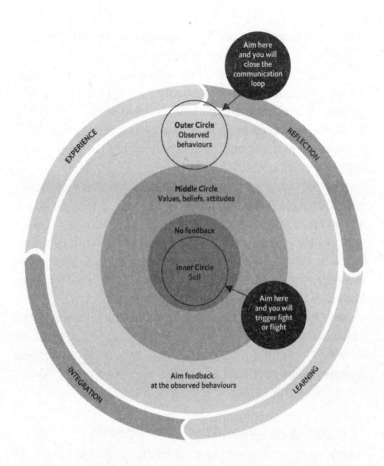

Figure 2. The giving good feedback framework

observe about people's behaviours and the impact of this behaviour on you and on the work you have to produce.

And, for your own development, you also need to be able to hear and understand the impact of the way you behave on your boss, your colleagues and the work you are producing together.

When you give (or receive) feedback at work, you are simply building on the communications skills you have been using in all other areas of your life.

You need to be able to do this in a way that supports people to move round the learning circle. When you receive feedback, you need to be able to ask enough questions to get the information you need to move to the next step.

The giving good feedback framework therefore focuses feedback on the behaviours people can see and change (the outer circle) rather than challenging their values, beliefs and attitudes (the middle circle) or commenting on people's personality and self-esteem (the inner circle).

As a result, it avoids the classic feedback problem of triggering a defensive reaction. Instead, it helps people to move round the circle via the key steps of experience, reflection, learning and integration, thus supporting progress and learning.

Remember

Feedback is always about communication. In a simple communication loop, it's the thing that closes that loop so that you know your message has been received and (hopefully) understood.

Communication is a skill we have been practising since the day we were born.

The more we understand what feedback really is, the more we'll feel comfortable about it and the more we'll improve at giving it.

Read on to learn more about why feedback really matters and learn new techniques for giving good feedback at work. But remember, it is always best to keep a simple, natural, human activity just that – simple.

In summary, feedback is:

- a natural human activity
- an activity we are all involved in, all the time, consciously and unconsciously
- an activity that should focus on things that go well, rather than only on things that go wrong
- an activity that should support learning
- always about clear, helpful, respectful communication between people, not just about process and systems. It is always focused on observed behaviours that the person can do something about.

2

Why does feedback matter?

"It is a truth universally acknowledged that a millennial in possession of a job must be in want of feedback."

Marcus Buckingham and Ashley Goodall[1]

Once upon a time, I supported a client who had been in a new job for a few weeks. The new job was career progression for Priya, involving her in daily decisions about how best to resource a big department store. It was a long-awaited dream. But after only a few weeks, she was considering leaving and asking her previous employer to take her back. Why?

Priya described her first day. She had been thrown straight in at the deep end, running the staff resourcing meeting. At the end of the meeting, she felt she had done well. At least, she felt she had got through the meeting without disgracing herself and she had some ideas of what she could do better next time.

"Sit down", the boss said, "and we will give you some feedback."

Priya noticed three other staff managers sitting with the boss. All four went through Priya's handling of the meeting in some detail. They commented on Priya's presenting style (too quiet), her method of asking for staff (not assertive), her manner (a bit wet), her decisions (foolish). Oh, and her sums were not good enough. (She hadn't noticed that the linen department's staff numbers were over the limit, so they could have been told to lend a member of staff to Christmas stationery. Now they had got away scot free. What was she thinking?)

Priya didn't know what to say. She wasn't thinking anything, really. It was her first day. She didn't know what to do with this onslaught of feedback about every aspect of a completely new task.

On the way home, she wondered why she had always thought feedback was so important. She felt guilty about the amount of time she had spent giving feedback to her six-year-old the previous day, when he had a new birthday toy that he didn't want to share with his friend. Perhaps that was reasonable behaviour, she thought, as he hadn't had the chance to play with it himself yet. It was rather like being given a load of feedback on how badly you are doing in the job you have only just started to do. She didn't feel like running the meeting again tomorrow. She was too afraid of the feedback.

After some consideration and discussion, she asked her previous employer if they would take her back. They were delighted. Priya was a valued employee, keen, quick to learn and very open to feedback.

Is feedback ever useful at work?

Like Priya, you may be keen to learn, to define what you mean by feedback and accept that feedback is particularly useful for small children, other people (and even occasionally for you).

However, I have had many clients with similar experiences of feedback as Priya, who question its usefulness at work after getting a ton of it all in one go. Others have had feedback delivered sporadically, many months after the event, which was just as categorically unhelpful. Even more clients have had well-meaning feedback, delivered on time, which still left them feeling demotivated and upset.

Opinions remain firmly divided about how useful feedback is at work. Research suggests that only 26% of employees find the feedback from their managers helpful.[2] A survey conducted by Jack Zenger and Joseph Folkman found that 44% of managers find giving negative feedback stressful or difficult, 21% of managers avoid giving negative feedback, and surprisingly, even more (37%) avoid giving positive feedback.[3]

There is one group apparently bucking this trend, the millennial generation of workers. This group is (allegedly) constantly asking for feedback in the workplace. They apparently view feedback as critical to their health and happiness as heating, clean drinking water and reliable Wi-Fi. Though even the existence of this feedback-loving group is disputed by some.[4]

So, is feedback a waste of time or a panacea for all development ills? Do some people have a problem with it just because of the way most organisations approach it or is there something fundamentally wrong with the concept of giving feedback? Should anyone be giving feedback at all? Does it matter?

These are not trick questions. As you would expect, because this is a book called *Giving Good Feedback*, I'm entirely with the (allegedly) feedback-loving millennials here. Yes, of course we should all be giving feedback. In fact, we should all get into the habit of giving feedback and asking for feedback at work.

And yes, feedback does matter. It matters very much

because feedback is all about communication and learning. As imperfect human beings, we all need help with:

- forward-looking feedback
- supporting development and growth
- making sense of new experiences
- moving us round the learning circle.

The paradox of feedback and humanity

Many presentations and training sessions on feedback start with a straw poll, asking people to tick the box that best describes their most likely response when they are asked, "Can I give you some feedback?"

Responses range from "Must you? It makes me anxious" to "I know it's good for me, but I'd rather not" or "I would prefer to have root canal treatment, without anesthetic."

All these feature a clear acknowledgement of the stress and anxiety caused by the question. It is this anxiety that demonstrates the paradox that we humans face when we receive feedback. You could also describe it as showcasing some of the limitations caused by our biological evolution.

There are many different worlds for human beings to navigate, both at home and at work. The skills and reactions required to survive in these different worlds (let alone thrive in them) have varied at different stages in our evolution.

Some of the natural reactions developed over the centuries to help human survival remain useful; others are a liability in contemporary situations. For example, for cavemen, the flight-or-fight reaction was useful to alert them to danger and get them ready to run away from woolly mammoths.

Now, the same primal reaction can overwhelm human beings in daily life, as we battle to suppress our responses. This is because when you are anxious, the same caveman stress reaction pops up. However, a caveman response is not usually appropriate for the modern workplace. Legging it out of the office, screaming "Run for your lives" and hurling a homemade wooden spear at the boss as you go is generally frowned upon.

There are a couple of other mechanisms we have developed, in the modern world, that are important stress responses. Cousins to flight or fight, these are "freezing" and "fawning". They are perhaps more socially acceptable for the workplace than fight or flight, but nonetheless damaging.

Freezing keeps you trapped in one place unable to process anything, whereas fawning (identified as a slightly later stress response than the other three) makes you obsequiously agreeable to any suggestion that someone makes.

So, when you arrive at work, someone asking "Can I give you some feedback?" has pretty much the same effect on your brain as spotting a dark shadow appearing round a corner or hearing stealthy footsteps behind you at night.

Your brain leaps into its primeval fight-or-flight state, and screams "Danger, danger". Then the fight- or-flight/freezing-or-fawning mechanism kicks in, flooding you with adrenaline. As a result, you will be completely unable to listen to what the person offering the feedback has to say. You will be too busy trying to run away.

The stress response occurs because feedback takes you away from your inner view of yourselves and forces you to realise that other people see you differently. Neuroscience has a lot to say about the impact of this.[5] Being forced out of your own, inner-world view is challenge enough. However, when processing feedback at work, this challenge is often heightened by the cumulative effective of poor feedback-giving in the world of work.

This is unfortunate, because developing and learning the skills appropriate for the world in which you find yourself is important. While you are learning, it is impossible to see yourself in action. You won't know how you come across to other people, and so you will not have a complete understanding of the impact of your behaviour on others.

Of course, you may be extremely clear about how you *intended* a particular comment to come across, what you *meant* to achieve or what you were *hoping* might be the result of your actions. However, whatever your *intentions* were, you are reliant on other people for feedback on how it landed with them. In other words, you need other people to help you see your blind spots or how you appear to the rest of the world.[6]

Take, for example, the Dunning–Kruger effect.[7] This posits that most people are likely to overestimate their abilities when they are not very good at something, and to underestimate what they are skilled at. Feedback is an essential part of reversing this tendency. For example, doesn't it feel great when someone tells you how much your warm, calm explanation of that medical procedure helped them understand it and get through it without too much trauma? Particularly if you had no idea this is how your communication style comes across.

Sometimes, of course, feedback is also painful: someone telling you, for example, that your communication has come across as superior and aggressive, even though you tried hard to have the opposite effect. When this happens, you have to go through the process of balancing your human need for approval and feeling accepted with your (also human) need to learn and to grow.

That is why feedback needs to be a dialogue. This gives the feedback space and time, enabling the people involved to share ideas and try them out. Then you can ask questions, understand the feedback, get over your initial sense of hurt and perhaps decide to take it on board. However, in many organisations, the sheer weight of data capture involved in the formal feedback process means this vital discussion stage is missed out. No one has the time or energy left for it.

Given all these complications, even though we may understand that it is important, is it possible to give useful feedback at work? If it is, how do we do it? Does it matter if we just give up and muddle through, doing our best, without the benefit of knowing what others think?

Who says feedback matters at work?

When considering why feedback matters at work, it's worth spending some time looking at the different approaches to giving feedback, and the arguments for and against it.

There is one school of thought that considers direct, immediate, tough feedback as being critical to an organisation's success. This is epitomised by Bridgewater Associates' CEO Ray Dalio.[8]

Then there is a completely opposing view, taken by Marcus Buckingham and Ashley Goodall who believe that such faith in feedback is nothing more than a fallacy.[9]

Alongside this thinking lies Kim Scott and her idea of

radical candour.[10] Scott favours direct feedback linked with compassion and careful relationship building.

Harvard professors Douglas Stone and Sheila Heen offer helpful insights from the perspective of receiving feedback.[11]

Let's look at these ideas in more detail.

Radical transparency

The idea of radical transparency is most readily associated with Ray Dalio and was enthusiastically taken up by many Silicon Valley employers, including Amazon and Netflix.

Dalio gathered his thoughts about his experiments in his book *Principles*, famously offering insights such as "no pain, no gain" and the idea that "tough love is both the hardest and the most important type of love to give".

Chief among his thoughts was the critical importance of employing radical truth and radical transparency to encourage open and honest dialogue and allow the best thinking to prevail. Linked to this was the idea that people cannot see themselves clearly and need to have problems pointed out to them.

For Dalio, most people see themselves as having two roles at work: one is the job itself and the other is making sure that they manage other people's impressions of them to make themselves look as good as possible. His view was that this led to a secretive environment, where people hide their own mistakes, and even cover up other people's, in case pointing these out leads to their own mistakes being exposed. At Bridgewater, he built on this idea, boasting that:

> we take things that ordinarily people would hide, and we put them on the table, particularly mistakes, problems and

weaknesses. We put these on the table, and we look at them together. We don't hide them.

In practice, that meant that staff were rated in real time, in a company meeting, using a set of criteria and "dot attributes". Staff had a "dot collector" app on their iPads, which had a list of their colleagues and a list of competencies to rate them against – such as management fundamentals or thinking qualities, broken down into attributes. The dot attributes included, for example: fighting to get in synch, willing to touch the nerve, logical reasoning, and seeing multiple possibilities.

As the meeting progressed, staff would busily rate their colleagues on these competencies, on a scale of 1 to 10, presumably also paying attention to the meeting. Dalio himself proudly revealed that he was unfavourably rated on at least one occasion, being rated a 3 on the competency "being assertive and open minded at the same time" by one young employee called Jen. ("What you are saying doesn't really make sense that much," she said, by way of justifying her rating.)

Dalio pointed to this as an example of the feedback system really working. His view was that people seeing their opinion as one of many on a screen (for example, while Jen was rating him a 3, another employee was rating him a 9 and he could see both ratings) shifted the conversation from arguing over opinions to "figuring out objective criteria for determining what opinions are best".

The system was enhanced with algorithms, which took what Dalio described as "believability" into account. This meant that the opinions of more believable people held greater weight than those of less believable people. Believability was based on those who had repeatedly proved their grasp of a given topic or management attribute. (Quite how this was assessed seems unclear; presumably, there were other algorithms to pick this up.)

Dalio clearly thought Jen had some reliable grasp of what being "assertive and open minded at the same time" meant and looked like in practice, because her feedback on this was put forward as an example of the system working.

Although Dalio's model was copied across Silicon Valley and beyond, it has also, perhaps unsurprisingly, led to criticism and debate. For Buckingham and Goodall, it has called into question the usefulness of feedback itself.

The feedback fallacy

In seeing feedback as a fallacy, Buckingham and Goodall explore the limits of feedback, arguing that it's not the route to improvement we might think it is and suggesting we dispense with the concept entirely.

They make three important points about Dalio's belief that the way to increase performance in companies is through rigorous, frequent, candid, pervasive and often critical feedback.

1. The idea of objectivity from other people is false, i.e. we are all subject to our biases and so are no better at providing this information objectively to other people than we are to ourselves.

2. Negativity is not useful. Talking about shortcomings hinders rather than helps learning.

3. There is no universal standard of excellence, so the approach of rating against a standard and giving feedback to match is deeply unhelpful.

Scientific evidence confirms the idea that, as human beings, we tend to evaluate information in a biased manner. Take, for instance, *confirmation bias*: the tendency to focus on evidence that confirms our beliefs and assumptions rather than looking for data that contradicts it.

Buckingham and Goodall posit that these biases mean that no one has the right to comment on other people's performance. Nor is it possible to reliably rate someone else's qualities, attributes or competencies. Buckingham points to the abstract nature of many of the concepts we are expected to give feedback about at work (for example, business acumen or Dalio's management fundamentals or thinking qualities) and suggests that it is impossible to hold these in our heads stably enough to rate one person on it and then immediately turn our attention to another teammate and rate them.

Instead, Buckingham believes that there are only three sources of input that are useful to team members.

Facts

Knowing facts about your job is helpful. It is always important to give people knowledge.

If someone doesn't know facts, it is appropriate to tell them: to explain how to do the job, provide technical knowledge on how an engine works, or what information to include in a press release, or detail the presenting symptoms of an illness.

Steps

There will be steps to follow to complete a task correctly or safely. If someone misses one, then it is appropriate to tell them. For example, for nurses, there are the correct steps to take to complete an injection safely. If one is missed, then it is entirely appropriate to say, "Don't ever miss that step again."

Reactions not feedback

In many work settings, though, it is impossible to have a universal standard of excellence. For example, there is no single way of giving a presentation, writing a memo, making a sale.

"The big fear of companies is misalignment and lack of control, which is understandable," Buckingham says. "The problem is that the value of a human being is the uniqueness of a human being. That's the value. That's the feature. Not something to be solved. Or try to fix."

All that other people can offer, he concludes, is a reaction to how something landed with them. So, people should stop saying, "Can I give you some feedback?" and instead say, "Here's my reaction."

Radical candour

Kim Scott disagrees with Buckingham and Goodall and, like Dalio, considers direct, truthful feedback to be critical to development in the workplace. She advocates "radical candour" as a management approach. But crucially, she also highlights the importance of bringing compassion and relationship-building into the feedback mix.

Scott acknowledges the usefulness of transparency with regard to business results. But she also points out that Dalio's approach does not play a part in fostering good working relationships, psychological safety or a productive, happy culture. Her view is that the word "radical" should indicate a management philosophy that is both new and completely different from what came before. The idea that bosses should use their power to behave like bullies is "old and banal" rather than new and radical.

Scott's view of feedback is that you give it because it is critical for the person to know. Not to make the effort to do so because we find it awkward is uncaring. In her book *Radical Candor* she likens this to telling someone they have spinach in their teeth – in Buckingham's parlance, feedback as steps or facts: just something the person needs to know.

The matrix she uses to summarise her thinking is reproduced in Figure 3. Across the two axes of challenge directly and care personally are different ways in which we give unhelpful feedback or avoid giving feedback at all: with ruinous empathy, obnoxious aggression and manipulative insincerity.

The sweet spot in the top right quadrant of Scott's matrix is described as "compassionate candour" (to avoid any confusion with the radical transparency movement), highlighting the importance of direct, caring feedback for both development and for the health of the company.

In her book, Scott describes two examples of particularly helpful feedback. One was when her boss gave her feedback on her performance in a presentation, insisting that she heard it and did something with it. Compassionate candour in action.

The other is a description of an employee, Bob, who was not doing his job well. Everyone liked him and did not want to upset him by giving him feedback about his performance. They all carried on making excuses for him and covering work he left undone. After Bob was fired, his complaint was, "Why did no one say anything?" Ruinous empathy writ large.

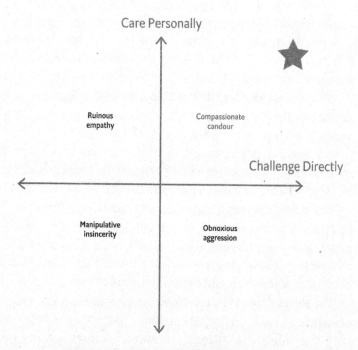

Figure 3. Kim Scott's compassionate candour[12]

Although Scott recommends giving feedback rather than leaving it unsaid ("Just say it!"), she draws a clear distinction with Dalio's approach of constant real-time feedback. She recommends picking your battles and leaving at least three things unsaid every day.

Thanks for the feedback

In their book *Thanks for the Feedback*, Douglas Stone and Sheila Heen move away from the common focus on training people to *give* rather than *receive* feedback. They point out how important it is to improve your skills in receiving feedback, and learn from it, even when (as the book's subtitle goes) it is "off base, unfair, poorly delivered, and, frankly, you're not in the mood". They suggest that feedback is critical to understanding the limitations and impact of your blind spots, and the way you see the world, relationships and communication.

To learn how to take on board and accept feedback, you need to focus on understanding yourself and take responsibility for your own reactions, rather than dismissing feedback because of limitations in the way it is delivered. The authors look in detail at things that can get in the way of receiving feedback well (such as truth, relationship and identity triggers) before thinking of ways to navigate around these so you can learn from any feedback offered.

The feedback fallacy turned around – why feedback really does matter

So there are a lot of different and interesting theories around feedback giving and how to approach it. But what does this all mean for feedback and why does it matter? Here's a clue.

Feedback really matters at work.

The idea of the feedback fallacy misses the point when suggesting that all we can do is react to someone else, and we cannot offer feedback because we can never be truly objective.

In Chapter 1, the key points involved in defining the term feedback were **information, opinion** and **reactions.**

Someone else's **opinion** or **reaction** is the **information** or starting point we need, to help us get in position on the learning circle.

We then start moving round the learning circle as a result

of the discussion about the **information** provided by the **reaction** or **opinion**.

The discussion gives you the opportunity to reflect, as you share more information and opinions, put your view across and get a better sense of what the other person has noticed.

Feedback is always an opinion, information that provides an important reflection of the impact that another person's behaviour has had on you. It is precisely this lack of objectivity, the fact that it is your viewpoint of their behaviour, that makes your feedback useful.

You are not talking about the impact they *intended* their behaviour to have on you. You are talking about the *actual* impact of whatever behaviour you have noticed, on you or on the work you are trying to produce. Your reactions to their behaviour.

So your reactions are, in fact, feedback and feedback is never an objective truth. This is exactly what makes it useful.

Consider an exchange that starts off like this.

Boss to Fergus: "Here's my reaction to the meeting. I noticed you asking Bill a lot of questions about the new product. This made me think that you don't know enough about the new product and its features to attend the sales meeting with the client. What's your take on that?"

Fergus can then explain what he meant to achieve by asking lots of questions.

Fergus to Boss: "Oh, I was trying to ask Bill about the plans for the launch of part two of the project. Then he started talking about the launch for part one. So I started asking questions, because I thought perhaps I had missed something."

Boss to Fergus: "Oh, I see. Yes, I'd forgotten that Bill didn't answer your first question."

Then Fergus and his boss can have a discussion about what he was trying to achieve and explore their views on how to get this across differently.

Good feedback at work matters even more

Let's think a bit more about the Bridgewater approach to feedback. Leaving aside the complexities of the Bridgewater ratings system, Dalio is right that we cannot see ourselves from the outside in the way others see us. Benjamin Franklin is often quoted in support of this, comparing the difficulty of "knowing oneself" with the hardness of a diamond or steel.

Psychology would seem to bear this out, with one study suggesting that 95% of us think we have strong self-awareness, but actually only about 10–15% of us actually possess it.[13] The more power we have, and the higher we rise in our careers, the less self-aware we might become. So Dalio is right again about the importance of soliciting feedback for himself from more junior staff members because feedback from others can help with this insight.

However, the brutal approach taken in radical transparency takes the concept of direct feedback to another level entirely and loses the key message in the giving good feedback framework: that feedback needs to be *helpful* if the recipient is to move around the learning circle.

Building on this, Scott raises some important points about how critical good relationships (or caring personally) are when considering why feedback matters – precisely because we find feedback stressful, whether we're giving it or receiving it. We have a deep need to be accepted by our social group as well as a need to learn and grow. Good feedback, given as part of a caring relationship, is the mechanism for meeting both these needs. The Bridgewater approach does not put enough focus on relationships for the feedback to be helpful.

Stone and Heen's focus on receiving, rather than giving, feedback is another useful approach as we consider how good feedback helps us around the learning circle. The power to decide what to do with feedback is always with the recipient. You may decide to learn something from it; or you may decide that it is misguided and wrong. Either way, you will have given yourself the best possible chance to learn and grow by engaging in the discussion and trying to understand where someone else is coming from.

When you join a company, there are lots of things you do not (in fact cannot yet) know. You will have many new experiences. You need feedback to help you understand how to negotiate these new experiences and learn from them. But you do not need to have all this feedback thrown in your face within your first hour at work, like Priya. Nor do you need a corporate culture that insists on pointing out every single fault you have, every minute of every day, as at Bridgewater.

But when you agree to take a job, you need to understand that this means you get paid for a certain number of hours a week. You may also need some help understanding your job specification, as it may list a load of duties that do not, on first glance, make complete sense or may be vague. (For example, "Duties may vary. Alongside other duties, the post-holder must also provide assistance to others when required.")

You may wonder how these requirements sit with having a boss who is always telling you to go that extra mile. How will you know what your job specification means? What are you actually required to do, every day? How will you know when you have done it well? How will you learn how to do it better?

Good feedback helps you see your behaviour through other people's eyes. Good feedback gives you both attention and the opportunity to learn: it meets one of your fundamental needs as an imperfect human.

For Priya, the feedback that finally pushed her into going back to her old employer came at the end of a long list of failings that needed to be put right.

"Also, by the way, we already have a Priya here, so your name just won't do. We'll call you Jasmine, shall we?"

Priya's previous employers had commented on how open she was to feedback. However, feedback about her name was a step too far. Priya's name had been bestowed on her at birth by her parents. This comment was therefore aiming right at the centre of the feedback model (her sense of self) not at behaviour or something she could do anything about. They could just as easily have told her to stop being so tall.

Everyone needs feedback to help them learn and grow, but feedback is never an objective truth. However, that doesn't mean it's not important. If you are to learn and grow, you need to be able to discuss and review the feedback you receive; to look at the examples of behaviour; to seek to understand and consider what you want to do about them.

Good feedback at work can help us learn. It matters.

What you decide to do with it is entirely up to you.

Remember

There are many theories about feedback.

- Feedback can be stressful, because of our limitations as human beings.
- Feedback is essential to our growth and development.
- Feedback is always another person's view or opinion. It is never objective.
- When feedback is a dialogue, it helps us learn and move around the learning circle.
- What we choose to do with feedback is up to each of us.

3

What makes feedback "good"?

"(Man's) errors are corrigible. He is capable of rectifying his mistakes, by discussion and experience. Not by experience alone."

John Stuart Mill[1]

After unilaterally renaming Priya as Jasmine, the team helpfully offered her more feedback at the end of the week.

"We all think you are very aggressive, Jasmine, and should be more open to criticism."

Of course, she could have taken the initiative, stopped them in their tracks and asked for examples of said behaviour. "What have you noticed I do that is making you describe me as aggressive? Could you provide me with some specific examples of behaviour?"

In the event she merely shouted, "I don't need any more feedback today, thanks. And my name is Priya! Get it right and back off!"

This was entirely her call. In the circumstances, I would say it was the right one. In Priya's position, Kim Scott would definitely have started to explain the concept of "obnoxious aggression" and told Priya to find the nearest exit.

Leaving aside the somewhat toxic nature of Priya's new organisation, however, giving good feedback takes some thought. As we have explored, a human desire for development and growth often conflicts with another deep human desire, to be loved and accepted just as we are. Not as our best selves, but as us on a bad day, tired, sick, hungover or sleep-deprived. Feedback at work that helps people to feel seen, understood, appreciated and totally accepted, just the way they are, is a big ask.

So when giving good feedback to others, there is a lot to think about if that feedback is to hit home and meet the needs of the recipient.

Douglas Stone and Sheila Heen refer to three different kinds of feedback we tend to give or expect at work:[2]

1. appreciation ("Thanks" or "That's great!")
2. coaching ("Here's a better way to do it")
3. evaluation ("Here's where you stand").

Problems can occur when the feedback offered is different to the recipient's expectations. In our earlier examples, if Andy had been expecting to be praised for his work with the Australian office and Mike was expecting to talk about how well the business was doing, there would be an initial shock as they were suddenly forced to realise that this was a different type of conversation altogether. The initial inability to process the feedback would be as much a result of mismatched expectations as of feedback not being carefully given.

In contrast, Priya was given all three types of feedback in one go, with an added sprinkling of criticism and judgement. Her new boss, on that first morning, should have spent some time getting to know Priya and building a relationship. Then she would have been able to work out how best to communicate with her, using this information to give appropriate, helpful feedback.

Priya's boss would then have followed one of the sacred tenets of how to give good feedback – remembering that feedback is all about *communication*.

Good feedback and communication

Let's go back to this point in detail. One of the activities often used at communication skills courses is to ask participants to come up with a list of adjectives to describe the way they generally prefer other people to communicate with them. Participants tend to include words like respectful, courteous, clear, warm, polite, concise, direct.[3]

If you were asked this question, what would you have on your list? I would hazard a guess and suggest you are unlikely to include adjectives like aggressive, rude, cold or brutal.

Strangely though, if I ask the same people to imagine communicating feedback at work in a way that could be described using the first set of pleasant adjectives, many of them struggle. When we delve into this further, it transpires that at work, when communicating feedback, they feel they need to communicate directly. They believe this is the only way to let people know where they stand. But they have no idea how to communicate directly in a polite way. And confronted with a choice between being direct or being polite, they end up barking harsh comments of the Ray Dalio ilk.

That's why, at work, many people are not communicating respectfully with other people in the way they themselves would like to be communicated with. Choosing this approach to communication turns feedback away from learning and into something unhelpful and damaging.

Let's be clear: there is absolutely nothing wrong with communicating in a direct manner. It is perfectly possible to communicate directly and remain polite. It is the way you interpret the term "direct" that is important.

When you are using the giving good feedback framework (see page 27), you will be communicating directly, clearly and well by focusing on:

- your reactions to the behaviours that people can change (the outer circle)
- rather than the inner core of people's personality and self-esteem (the inner circle), which they cannot change
- the impact that these behaviours have on you
- the impact on the work you are trying to do.
- You will then spend some time discussing these reactions with the person you are talking to.

As a result, you will be closing the communication loop.

Good feedback is not just criticism

Unfortunately, the feedback that often sticks in your mind is the feedback that you struggle to know what to do with. It leaves you feeling confused or attacked in some way.

In other words, bad feedback goes to the heart of your personality, generalising about traits or attacking inherent attributes that you can do nothing about. For example, "You are slow/stupid/lazy. You are useless. We think you are aggressive. You always ..."

This sort of comment is often what people mean when they talk about direct feedback. It is direct in the sense that it offers a definite label or judgement. But offering labels and judgements pushes people into flight-or-fight mode. It makes them close down rather than remain open to learning. This is because it is aimed at their innermost core and is about something that is difficult for them to change. It challenges their sense of self.

It is certainly not polite. And it does not help anyone learn. Judgements and labels are always a hindrance rather than a help.

They also tend to be critical. One of the reasons why people find the terms "direct" and "polite" contradictory is that they have learnt to associate direct feedback with criticism.

The horseman shouting, "Yet another stupid thing you've done in the space of half an hour, you complete ****wit" was not unusual at the time. I like to think that we are more enlightened now and would simply dismiss this as bullying behaviour. But it's a style of communication that has not entirely left the world of work.[4]

As you start to work through the giving good feedback framework, remember that "good feedback" is not the same as "criticism".

Clear feedback is one thing. Brutal commentary, finding fault, apportioning blame, concentrating on everything that has gone wrong, are all something else entirely.

If you are struggling to give direct feedback in a polite way using this model, another question to ask yourself is, "How is this helpful?"

Good feedback should always be helpful. So instead of saying, "If you can't say anything nice, don't say anything at all," we could say, "If you can't say anything helpful, don't give feedback at all."

Margaret Heffernan expounds the importance of good, helpful feedback and backs this up with a tremendously evocative analogy.[5] She recounts the tale of an experiment (the Muir superchicken research) in which a group of chickens were divided into two groups: a top breeding group, who were kept separately; and a control group, who were left alone, to mix and carry on with their chicken lives freely.

The top breeding group turned out to be top breeders merely because they were overcompetitive. They ended up pecking each other to death. The control group did much better. From this Heffernan extrapolates that too much critical and brutal feedback is the work equivalent of being pecked to death by rival chickens.

If we want to support each other to learn and thrive, we have to focus a little less on behaving like chickens and a little more on being helpful.

Blame plays an important part in unhelpful criticism disguised as feedback. One of the reasons why the four horsemen were afraid to discuss feedback was because they were used to being blamed for things. Learning from mistakes wasn't something they understood. Pointing out what was wrong and apportioning blame for a mistake was an enthusiastic pastime for the whole company. But that was as far as it went. The idea of offering helpful feedback to support people round a learning circle, to help them grow and develop, was completely foreign to them.

Just as you are not going to improve your relationships at home by following your partner around the house, offering a brutal, negative commentary on their vacuuming skills, nobody at work is going to improve anything when subjected to the same treatment.

Answering the question "How is this helpful?" with the response "It will make me feel better, because it passes on the blame" may be entirely human. However, I am not going to give you permission to hand over that feedback.

This is because, although it may feel tremendously therapeutic for you, it will not be helpful for the other person. Blame has no place in good feedback.

Much better to behave a little less like chickens, and think again. Ask yourself, "What can I say about the impact of that person's behaviour on me, the work or the team, that will be helpful for them? What will help them learn?"

Stories and feedback

At the beginning of this book, I mentioned that everything to do with feedback starts with a story. This is because human intelligence is organised around stories.[6]

When you make comments focused on the middle of the circle – "Aisha is a bit lazy" or "Pablo isn't very keen, he's not a team player" – this is because you have noticed some behaviour and have used it to tell a story about that individual. These comments are natural for you, as a human, to make. However, they are not good feedback. One of the reasons why it can be a shock to get feedback is that you suddenly realise that other people are using information about you to make up a story about you that is inaccurate (in your view).

You may find you do this, for example, when someone does not follow your instructions. ("There he goes again, useless, never listens.") At this point, you need to check yourself and the story you have made up, by having a discussion about what you actually noticed. Instructions are necessary to perform any job and will generally form the prelude to feedback, because the way people carry them out will require further comment and discussion.

A reaction to the data you have gathered about the way someone appears to have failed to follow your clear instructions (in *your* view) may lead another discussion that clarifies your instructions that are not clear (in *their* view). If instructions do not seem to be followed first time round, it is important that you seek some feedback on your instructions – that is, check the clarity of your communication.

This will help you ensure that you have closed the communication loop, and your message has been received and understood. Priya could have done with some instructions on how to run the meeting, for example, before being offered feedback on how she approached it first time round. It is hard to accept and learn from feedback if there were no clear instructions in the first place.

A variation on the Fergus/Boss exchange, in the case of instructions, could go like this.

Boss to Fergus: "I noticed that you did not use the checklist I asked you to follow for this task. Tell me what else you need me to explain about the checklist."

Fergus: "I did tell you that I did not know where the checklist was. You told me to ask Mai, so I did. She told me that nobody has been able to locate that checklist for years. I did not know who else to ask."

Boss: "I see. What got in the way of you coming back to ask me?"

Fergus: "I was frightened to ask you. I thought the way you told me to go and find the checklist meant you did not want me to ask you any more questions."

At some point, once Fergus actually does have the checklist to refer to, the boss can move on to offering more reactions to the way he has carried out his variety of instructions.

Boss to Fergus: "Following a checklist means you need to tick the boxes to show what steps you have followed. If you don't do this, I can't check what has been done and what is still left to do."

At some stage, these instructions will change into a range of feedback conversations for coaching, evaluation or appreciation (to use Stone and Heen's terms).

Either way, if you are using the good feedback model you will always be commenting **from your perspective** on what behaviours you observed and the impact of the behaviours on you or on the work the person is doing. Your perspective may be in comparison with a checklist or procedures of how to do the job, but it will still be your perspective of what you think you have seen.

It will still be good feedback, because it will give the person the opportunity to reflect on your reaction, decide what they want to do with that information and then try something new. Or to ask you questions if it still isn't clear or if they have misinterpreted what you want. Or check with someone else if they think you are talking rubbish. In this way, they will start to move round the learning circle.

Of course, if they are like Fergus and have a problem with the general concept of a checklist, there may need to be some rather more difficult conversations further down the line. But we can come to these later in the book.

Relationships at work

To give good feedback at work, you need to build good relationships. Not all of us find relationship building easy. Look at what can happen in the average family when someone dies and there are arguments over who inherits what. Or how we can get tied up in knots when we try to agree plans for important family occasions or religious celebrations. All sorts of buried resentments and issues can appear.

If we find it hard to give our brother or sister feedback about the impact on us of the selfish way they always refuse to come home for Christmas or Thanksgiving, or the cavalier way they handle our elderly mother's finances, how can we be expected to give feedback to an employee who has not managed to follow simple instructions?

Fortunately, our relationships at work are based on different criteria to our relationships at home. We can "care personally" and build relationships, but we can do this without the complex dynamics and undercurrents of long-buried sibling rivalries or parental issues. The link that applies to both work and home relationships is the link between good communication and good feedback. Communication skills are something we all need to develop throughout our lives. And because feedback at work is so important, building communication skills and using them to forge the relationships required to enable good feedback is critical. Happily, with enough time, practice and effort, everyone is perfectly able to communicate better.

Communication and observed behaviours

At work, you are managing staff who have a contract for their labour, which is offered in return for pay. You too are offering your own labour, with an agreed contract, in return for pay.

This is clearly different to your relationships at home. You only have the right to offer feedback at work on the behaviours you observe that you feel have an impact on you and the work you are producing as a team. These can be behaviours that have a positive or a negative impact on you, the work or the team. Equally, your manager and the people you work with have the right to offer you feedback on these areas.

In both circumstances, feedback will be aimed entirely at the **observed behaviours**, shown in the outer circle of the model, not offering judgement on values, beliefs and attitudes, not attacking the way they are (i.e. their sense of self) and not commenting on their personality.

Focusing on observed behaviours and your reactions to them takes some of the emotion out of the equation. It thus avoids the classic feedback problem of triggering an immediate defensive reaction and provides a better starting point to help people move round the learning circle.

Let's look in more detail about how Brian handled remote feedback to Andy about his attitude and the impact of his behaviour.

He will have raised Andy's hackles by opening the conversation with a comment about his attitude. This is dangerously close to the middle of the circle, to the core of

Andy's personality and self-esteem. "You've got a bad attitude" feels like one of those vague, ego-based comments that people get easily labelled with in places like work or school.

A better approach would have been for Brian to start the conversation with a comment on the behaviour he observed from Andy in the previous day's meeting. He could then have pointed out that this was similar to his behaviour in many other meetings over the years, behaviour he had previously tried to discuss with Andy. So Andy would be helped round the learning circle like this.

The learner (Andy) has a concrete experience (a new experience or a reinterpretation of an existing experience).

- Brian says something to Andy that comments on his behaviour. For example: "In the meeting yesterday, you told me I didn't know anything about the work in the Australian office. When you speak to me like that, I feel disrespected."

The learner (Andy) reflects and observes the new experience (any inconsistencies between experience and understanding are of particular importance).

- Andy asks why Brian feels differently today about his plain speaking. He has never complained before.
- Brian explains that he has noticed the same behaviour several times and tried to discuss it with Andy before. Andy usually laughs it off. This leads him to believe that Andy is not listening to him or taking the feedback seriously.

The learner (Andy) has new ideas as a result (abstract

conceptualisation, where reflection gives rise to the new idea or modification to an existing abstract concept).

- Andy is surprised and shocked that Brian has thought like this about him for a while. He thinks about it, chats to his wife, realises that not everyone appreciates his humour, and that he should think before he speaks.

The learner (Andy) actively experiments (applying these ideas to the world about them to see the results).

- Andy gets some coaching support. He practises how to apologise and asks Brian for a second chance. He explains that he hadn't realised how Brian was interpreting his behaviour. Now that he has understood, he will try a different way of communicating with him. He says he would be grateful if Brian could feedback specific information on how this comes across. Then he can practise and learn new ways of communicating. Brian agrees to give him a final chance.

Reflection and dialogue

When using this model, an important step is to give time and space for reflection and discussion. It is also what can make giving feedback remotely more difficult. It is hard to sit in silence at any time, even harder when you are both staring at a screen, trying to gather your thoughts after giving some feedback. How long are you supposed to wait?

Faced with a choice between waiting in silence or just delivering the message, saying, "Okay, well, bye then," and hitting the end meeting button on Zoom, many managers hit the button. But building in time for dialogue and reflection is important. Sometimes you have to do this in an overt, practical way. For example, "Is your screen frozen or are you just thinking?"

If this feels too challenging, a better option would be to suggest someone takes a bit of time to think through the feedback you've just given them remotely, and then convene another Zoom meeting to discuss it.

When watching someone do a presentation for the first time, for example, most of us would not dream of shouting comments like "Rubbish slides!", "Too fast!", "Now it's too slow!", "Boring!" This in fact was what happened (via technology) using Dalio's radical transparency model of real-time feedback.

This is not good feedback because it gives no time for either the giver or receiver to reflect, for the feedback to be couched in terms of behaviour, or for a dialogue about the reaction or observation. ("What do you mean – too fast? What should I do differently? Do I just have to speak slower? How? I always talk quickly when I am nervous. Or do you mean I'm giving too much information too quickly? How do I change that, right now, in the middle of the presentation?")

When we are learning, trying something new, we are focusing on our learning process, concentrating on the steps we need to take to perform a task: first I do this, then I do that.

Our brains can't be in more than one place at once, so moving from the learning process to working out what someone means if they shout "Boring!" is impossible. We will get stuck at this point; no learning or movement round the circle is possible.

Focusing on behaviours means you have to explain what you see and talk about its impact. Discussing your feedback (or reaction) to the impact on you of behaviours that people can change, closes the communication loop – and opens up the dialogue needed.

After that presentation, for example, feedback such as "The beginning was too fast" is not enough to help the person move round the learning circle. Instead, you might open a feedback dialogue with something like, "Here's my reaction. At the beginning of the presentation, you talked quickly and flicked through ten slides. This made it hard for me to follow all the ideas and take them in."

The listener can then take this on board, and you can discuss what might work better. Practise slowing right down at the beginning, for example, if this is when they tend to be nervous, or focus on a few key slides to illustrate and anchor the main points.

Perhaps more importantly, positivity can be king in learning. Giving feedback does not always mean pointing out what is wrong. If we are talking about our experience of the impact of a person's behaviour, giving feedback on what has gone well is often more useful than on focusing on what went wrong. For example, with the presentation example, you could comment on the person's excellent response to questions at the end of the presentation.

> "I noticed when you were answering questions that you spoke at a pace that was great for me to follow and understand. The way you smiled and looked directly at each person you responded to really built a rapport with the audience. This had the impact of making it easy for me to listen and connect with what you were saying."

Then you can use this positive example to consider how you can take parts of what worked to develop their approach at the beginning of the presentation, when they are more nervous.

Let's go back to our giving good feedback framework and recap what ingredients go into giving good feedback. As we have already discussed, feedback is always about communication.

1. In a simple communication loop, it's the thing that closes that loop so you know your message has been received and (hopefully) understood.

2. When closing that communication loop, you are talking about the impact of that person's behaviour on you, what you saw, what impact you consider it may have had on outcomes (such as a project you are working on together). This is very important. You are not offering a universal objective truth that must be accepted as such. You will not have the whole story, and it is important that you offer your feedback in this spirit.

3. You also need to build in some space and time for the person to consider what you have said, and to discuss it, before they decide what to do with your feedback. As part of this dialogue, you will hear their side of the story, which may alter your view and put your feedback in a different perspective.

4. Good feedback means regular, helpful communication about specific behaviour, not constantly slapping people in the face with criticism. Some people need feedback more often than others.[7] But most of us, like Priya, can only cope with so much feedback at any one time.

Remember

- The giving good feedback framework aims feedback at observable behaviours and the impact of these behaviours on you, the work required and the team.

- Feedback aimed at observable behaviours and their impact supports movement around the learning circle.

- Feedback should also focus on what goes well and not just on what goes wrong.

- Good, clear communication and discussion are vital to the learning process – and are therefore essential elements of feedback.

PART 2

What gets in the way?

What information have you picked up so far? Have you tried out anything new at work as a result? Why not do a review of your learning at this point? Practise giving yourself some feedback on how you feel you have made use of the information you have read.

Just to jog your memory, by this stage in the book, you should:

- have a clear definition of the term feedback
- understand the power feedback can have
- be able to articulate why feedback is important
- have developed some ideas about how to give good feedback.

But don't panic if you have the horrible feeling there are still many unacknowledged skeletons lurking in the depths of your cupboard. By unacknowledged skeletons, I mean feedback that you have not yet managed to give to members of your team.

Perhaps you have shied away from it for so long that it has withered away. You can no longer remember what it looked like in the flesh, and you are unable to bring it to life for long enough to discuss it. There it lurks, causing you stress, just waiting to fall out of your office cupboard at the least opportune moment.

It is quite normal to feel like this. That's why Part 2 focuses on you, and what gets in the way when you try to give or receive feedback. This is important, because the feedback you give says as much about you as it does about the recipient.

This section will review theory and opinions around the

barriers to giving good feedback at work, including personal experience and style, bias and organisational culture.

One of the key questions to consider in this section is, "Am I really giving feedback?"

Or am I saying, "Why aren't you more like me?"

Questions to yourself

Before you plunge into this section, consider your personal experience and style, your biases and the organisational culture you work in. You might want to make some notes in answer to the following questions.

- What situations have you had recently when you tried to give good feedback and felt you had failed?
- What barriers did you face?
- What factors got in the way?

Read on to find out more.

4

Personal experience and style

"You have to know who you are, who you think you are, who your neighbours think you are. You must talk the truth about yourself. Otherwise, life is just a waste of time, isn't it?"

Quentin Crisp[1]

The health and safety officer appears in my office in a panic. There has been an accident at work, involving a wheely office chair, a Myers–Briggs personality report and two training and development managers. I am not sure if it is a joke or a serious catastrophe, but I am not allowed to run to the scene, lest I cause another accident.

It turns out that the senior manager (Elaine) sat down suddenly on an office chair that had rather well-oiled wheels. So well oiled that she shot across the room, narrowly avoiding serious injury. The junior manager, Nour, is crying and blaming herself. The health and safety officer is sure this needs to be recorded as an accident at work, and hovers anxiously with the accident book while I try to work out what has gone on.

It seems that Elaine (relatively new to the organisation) wanted to give Nour some super-helpful feedback on the importance of professional development. Nour is resistant to feedback (from Elaine), so Elaine decided to discuss their Myers–Briggs personality types.[2] She thought this would depersonalise the discussion and make it more objective.

The accident occurred when Elaine waved a Myers–Briggs report she had completed earlier under Nour's nose, saying she thought it was obvious that Nour was an INTP (Introverted, iNtuitive, Thinking, Perceiving). Nour pushed the report away, rather more vehemently than she meant to, leading to Elaine sitting down suddenly and then sailing away across the room.

What is wrong with Nour? Why doesn't she want Elaine's carefully thought through, super-helpful feedback? Why is she so angry with her well-meaning colleague?

Both managers believe wholeheartedly in the concept of feedback and spend a lot of time running developmental training sessions. But this particular relationship is not working. Plus, Nour points out that Elaine is not really all that well meaning or helpful in the way she comes across.

"The problem isn't our personality types," she says. "It's the fact that she is so aggressive, patronising and bossy all the time."

Feedback is all about you

You may be very aware that giving good feedback is important. You may also grudgingly accept that you are not perfect and appreciate receiving feedback from time to time. However, you can still find it extremely hard both to give and receive feedback, without quite understanding why. And why some people, giving you some types of feedback, can push your buttons more than others.

How many of us have dismissed feedback such as,

"Everybody in the office thinks you are not a team player, Gerry" as unhelpful? How often have you offered feedback phrased like this and been surprised when people don't take on board your wise offerings about their limitations?

This is because the factors that make feedback so important are the same things that get in the way. Everyone brings their own baggage into the workplace, and it is this baggage you notice when feedback first confronts you with a self you do not recognise.[3]

Your personal baggage includes:

- your personality, preferences and values
- the impact of your personal experience and cultural background
- the stories you tell yourself
- your communication style.

All of these can pop up when you least expect and get in the way of receiving and giving good feedback.

Of course, you won't always recognise the self that is reflected back to you via feedback. It may not be a self you want to accept or welcome into your world view – even if everyone in the team agrees that the feedback you don't like is the accepted wisdom in the office about who you are and how you operate.

You are, of course, always free to decide just to take yourself (and, for example, your lack of being a team player) elsewhere, where your many other positive traits are appreciated. Their loss, not mine, you might think, a shade bitterly.

However, you might have also lost something by rejecting the (possibly) clumsy, unfair feedback outright. Even badly presented feedback about the way you are perceived may be useful. In the example above, both Nour and Elaine have their own ideas about the way they come across to others. Elaine thinks she is super helpful and that Nour is disrespectful and resistant. Nour thinks she is intuitive and empathetic, and that Elaine is superior and condescending.

Who is right? In reality, they both are. Feedback is always about two people. Elaine and Nour are both skilled in their different ways and can learn a lot from each other. Look at their different approaches to training. Elaine is interested in models and reads a lot about management theory. Nour has a more instinctive approach, which she considers more suitable for their very practical clients. They could both use elements of each. If they could discuss and share their approaches in detail, this would be helpful for both of them.

They are unlikely, though, to discover this if they don't have a discussion about their different reactions or feedback to each other. Sometimes feedback that you believe is wrong, really is wrong. But sometimes it can uncover a blind spot in what you know about yourself.[4] And this is what makes you uncomfortable.

So when you receive feedback that you think is wrong, work hard, through discussion, to communicate and understand where the other person is coming from. You can still decide to ignore it and move on. But you may be surprised with what you learn.

And what about the times when you offer perfectly good feedback to someone else and it is not received well?

The intentions gap

How many times have you sat in a café, watched a couple talking and tried to work out what they are saying? Are they having an argument or a loving conversation? How can you tell? You will be picking up information by scanning their eyes and the shape of their mouths. Are they looking at each other; are they are frowning or smiling?[5]

At work, your colleagues will be doing the same thing as they try to work out what mood you are in, what you really believe about a topic. You may be trying hard to behave in a supportive and helpful way but your face and your voice may betray you if you really have other values and emotions. This sort of mismatch can also get in the way when you try to offer feedback.

Chapter 2 explored the difference between intention and the way your behaviour actually lands with the person concerned. Feedback is a useful tool to help you address this gap.

The same gap can exist when offering feedback to other people. Like Elaine, people tend to focus on their intentions. Elaine genuinely believes she is being super helpful in giving this feedback. She feels she has experience to offer and has Nour's best interests at heart.

Elaine does really have an awful lot of useful information about training models which could be useful learning for Nour. However, she is also entirely unaware of the wrestling that is going on in her own head.

In her relationship with Nour, much about Elaine's world view is being challenged. For a start, she believes fervently in the importance of professional qualifications. Since Nour does not have as many of these as Elaine, she does not think Nour deserves her good reputation with the management team.

Elaine is not as confident as she looks. She is new to the organisation, and negotiated a big pay rise she is not entirely sure she deserves. She also feels a bit lonely. In fact, she is slightly threatened by Nour's close working relationships. When Elaine feels insecure, she retreats into judgement mode to make herself feel better. Nour, she decides, is too emotional and not as professional in her dealings with people.

Nour, Elaine reasons, is therefore, lucky to have a super-thoughtful colleague like herself to point this out. Even though she may not be aware of all the judgements she is making as a result of her world view, Elaine will betray these to Nour through her voice (which she cannot hear in the same way that Nour hears it) and her face (which she cannot see).

Nour can see Elaine's judgements all too clearly and therefore does not take her "best intentions" argument on board. She is also very busy batting off her own baggage, related to her own world view, and does not ask questions to try and get past this.

It turns out that Elaine's manner reminds Nour of her early experiences when she arrived in the United States as a refugee. Patronising officials waved all sorts of official forms at her and gave her various labels to mark her immigrant status. Partly because of this and partly because she sees herself as an empathetic, intuitive person, Nour considers the idea of a test and label for her personality an insult. Plus, she is tired of Elaine talking a lot of management jargon. She thinks Elaine does this to appear more knowledgeable and rub in the fact that she went to Harvard, whereas Nour worked her way up to her training manager position, gaining her qualifications part time. So she dismisses Elaine and her feedback, labelling her as aggressive, patronising and bossy.

As a result, they have both headed off far too far down the "rabbit hole of intentions" to return to a helpful feedback discussion.[6] This is a shame – they could both learn a lot from listening to each other.

Personal experience

Just like Nour, dealing with memories and experiences that impact the way she is hearing Elaine's proffered feedback, you will have some experiences that get in your way.

What feedback have you received that sticks in your mind? It might be a teacher commenting on an essay you wrote at school. A partner or relative talking about the impact of the way you behaved with a mutual friend at a group dinner. Was it positive or negative feedback? What were they commenting on? What did they say? What did they do? How did they break it down?

Chances are, if you remember it as a positive experience, it was forward looking and constructive. It probably did not send you into fight-or-flight mode. You can build on this when giving feedback to others. If not, there might be some relearning to do.

Schools, for example, are prolific in evaluation-type feedback and for many people this is where they have their first experiences of feedback. Elaine remembers a school report that said she "lacked coordination" in tennis lessons. In adult life, this means she breaks into a cold sweat whenever the idea of a corporate away day including any kind of sports is mooted.

One of the CEOs I work with remembers the comment, "Charlie is unlikely to amount to anything with his poor organisational skills and lack of can-do attitude." He is now very sensitive to any suggestion that his calendar is not up to date, and has gained the nickname "Tigger" because he is never anything less than stratospherically positive.

A coaching client remembers proudly presenting his school report to his parents, pointing out the grade A he had received for art. His parents grabbed the report, saying, "But what did you get for maths? And the other *useful* subjects?" He is still working his way through a painful career switch from accountancy to graphic design.

All your early experiences of feedback, however well intentioned at the time, have an impact on how you respond to feedback now. They will also affect the things you are likely to focus on when you give feedback to others.

However, none of us wants to stay stuck due to a negative early experience. At some stage you have to stop blaming your parents, grow up and take responsibility for your own actions and development.[7]

At work, we have to do the same. We have to (metaphorically) grow up, cast off shadows from previous influences and take responsibility for our own development. Delightful though it may be to blame our managers for their limitations, or our juniors for their lack of ability, the reality is that every relationship will involve two people. The person you can have the most influence over is yourself. It is therefore worth spending time exploring your own experiences and thinking about what you can do to make sure they do not trip you up when you least expect it. In other words, how you can keep bridging that inevitable gap.

Relationships and feedback

You know that relationships are important to giving good feedback.

If you find *receiving* feedback difficult, a good place to start is the relationship (or lack of it) between you and the other person. You will listen happily to feedback from people you respect and have a good relationship with. You will not find that so easy with people whom you think do not know you, understand you, or have any idea about how to do your job. This is not necessarily because the feedback is unhelpful but (as with Elaine and Nour) the relationship generates so many unhelpful associations that you are not able to hear it from that person.

Not all communication loops are helpful. It's easy to get stuck in an unhelpful, reinforcing communication loop, where each person in the relationship is doing things to perpetuate an unhelpful dynamic.

The best way to diffuse a difficult relationship, like the one between Elaine and Nour, is to think about the part each of you plays and what each of you is contributing to the problem.

Think about a conversation you have had that has not worked for you. A feedback conversation, for example, where you had your breath taken away by the sheer unfairness of the feedback you were offered. Rather than blaming the other person for not being able to communicate, you could try to work out what was going on for you. You never know, the feedback might actually be useful. And the only thing you can have any control over is yourself.

So stop yourself from immediately rejecting that terribly unfair feedback from that useless manager. Take a minute to think. Why did you find that conversation so difficult?

Categories of conversation

As a useful starting point, Stone and Heen offer three conversation categories to consider.[8] What sort of conversation is this? Does it match one of these three types of conversation?

1. **What happened?**
   – a disagreement about what happened or should happen, who said what, and who did what
2. **Feelings**
   – emotions and feelings get in the way
3. **Identity**
   – an internal debate over whether this feedback means you are competent or incompetent, a good person or bad person.

If you can match your conversation to one of these categories, you can then ask yourself some relevant questions and review your own contribution to the difficulty.

- **What happened?**
  Do you know exactly what the other person observed? What do they think happened? Discuss it with them. Get a sense of their perspective. Can they turn the feedback into descriptions of behaviour?
  Review this and then you can get into discussing your different reactions to the behaviours and the impact on each of you.

- **Feelings**
  How do you feel about it? What is going on with your emotions? Do you think your feelings are valid? Are they appropriate? Are they really about something else? Should

you acknowledge or deny them? What do you do about the other person's feelings?

Review this and then you can each acknowledge the impact of the other person's behaviour, in terms of feelings, on each of you.

- **Identity**

What other nerves has this feedback touched? Has it upset your world view, your story about the sort of person you are? By someone pointing out that you forgot to deal with an admin detail, do you feel your identity as an organised person is threatened?

Review this, and then, if you can get a clear description of the behaviour the other person has noticed and the impact on them, or on the work, then you can decide what to do with it. Perhaps you can both just focus on the issue they are giving feedback on (an admin detail) rather than building it into something bigger.

This list is, of course, just a starting point. These things are complex. A lot goes into building our world view. So when feedback threatens it, untangling it is complex too.

The stories you tell yourself

Research conducted at Stanford University looks at the concept of identity stories and posits that everyone has one of two different versions.[9] These have a significant impact on the way people experience criticism, challenge and failure and, in turn, affect the way they give and receive feedback.

One identity story assumes that traits are **fixed.** As a result, you believe that any feedback you get reveals "how you are".

You believe that you are unable to change fixed traits, so consequently there is a lot at stake. This means it is hard to receive any feedback constructively.

Nour has built up an identity as a self-made woman. She believes she is good at her job mainly because of her instinctive empathy and experience. But she is insecure about her lack of qualifications. A colleague offering her feedback that she needs to "use more business models to appear more professional" will have a big impact on her.

Her thoughts might run along the following lines. "I won't be successful if I do not use these models. Does this mean she is telling me I'm not good at my job? I've always thought I am good at my job. Am I wrong? Should I look for another one before I get fired?"

The other identity story assumes that traits are **not fixed,** and you can always change and grow. As a result, you perceive feedback as valuable information about where you are now and what to work on next. Consequently, it is a welcome input rather than an upsetting verdict that you can do nothing about. This means it is easier to use the feedback constructively, which leads to a growth mindset.[10]

Clearly the wrong mindset can get in the way of us giving (and receiving) good feedback. However, changing your mindset is not easy. Carol Dweck, professor of psychology at Stanford University, looks at different techniques to help change your reactions.[11]

One technique she suggests is *affect labelling*. This involves putting our feelings into words. For example, instead of pushing Elaine away on the wheely chair, Nour could have said,

"I'm surprised and honestly a bit scared by you waving that report at me. Can I take a few minutes before we discuss anything?"

When she had recovered, she could have said,

"I am uncomfortable with labels. Could we discuss a real-life example of something I am doing that you feel needs to change and is getting in the way of the way we work together? Then we can discuss the impact of you approaching feedback for me in this way."

You might be thinking that nobody talks like that in your organisation. But if you feel something is getting in the way of you giving (or receiving) good feedback, consider the following points.

- Find something you can say to buy yourself some time to consider what is going on for you. For example, "That's interesting, thanks. Let me think about it and we can discuss it a bit more."

- Use this time to work out what you want to ask about, or how to put your reservations into words.

- Discuss this with someone outside the situation if this feels too hard for you to do alone.

- Remember, two things can be true at the same time (for example, Elaine can be behaving in a bossy way, *and* she can also have some useful insights for Nour). Nour can work out what the triggering points are about Elaine's behaviour, set them aside and then look at what she can learn from the feedback.

Another approach that Dweck recommends is to practise *self-affirmation*: reminding yourself that there are other aspects to your identity than the one currently being considered. Nour could have reminded herself of the voluntary work she does at the local youth group, where she has built helpful, supportive relationships with troubled youngsters. Dweck's research shows that this helps people feel less threatened and so inhibits the flight-or-fight mechanism that is a common reaction when hearing threatening feedback. As a result, you can be more open to listening.

Of course, you are not obliged to take the feedback on board; you can decide what you want to do with it at a later stage, when you have everything in perspective. Nour could have reminded herself of all the experience she has and how useful this could be to Elaine but remained open to new ideas and different ways of doing things. Elaine's idea of looking at their different personalities using Myers–Briggs or considering using different communication styles could then have been a useful way for the two of them to frame their relationship.

Clarity, culture and communication styles

I once joined a school workshop on how to discourage bullying. The teacher told the children, if they were faced with behaviour they didn't like in the playground, to chant, "Stop it, I don't like it."

I asked my daughter afterwards if she found it a useful technique.

"No," she said, flatly. "I've no idea why they think that works. I mean, have they *even been* in the playground lately?"

In saying this, she essentially exposed the limitations of the many tips and strategies for good communication expounded in books like this one. Does anybody actually talk like that? How well do those tips translate into the world of work? It's more complicated, isn't it? I mean, have I *even been* in the workplace lately?

I have, and I found myself wondering how easy it would be to offer the comment, "Stop it, I don't like it" to a boss at work, let alone explain why.

And that's reasonable bosses, by the way, never mind the ones who send you emails with the subject heading "Yet another stupid thing you've done in the space of half an hour you complete ****wit".

(Clearly when dealing with these bosses, you just report them to human resources, rather than waste time trying to improve their behaviour. Nobody should ever have to put up with behaviour they don't like. We have come a long way in understanding the negative effects of bullying in the workplace, as well as at school.)

Feedback, as we know, is all about communication. But the key point here is that communication is complex. It is not always easy just to say it, as Kim Scott would have us believe. Sometimes it can be hard to communicate the most basic of our likes and dislikes, for a whole range of reasons.

When you think about what gets in the way of you giving feedback, you are also considering what might get in the way of you communicating clearly. Respectful, clear communication helps in giving and hearing clear, respectful feedback. But everyone has different communication styles, and they all impact us differently. Communication that one person finds direct and upsetting may just be clear to another. Feedback to a school bully may get them to back off or make the situation a lot worse. A great deal can depend on how it is delivered.

Michael Ivanov's study in behavioural communication explores the idea that that people communicate different feelings, needs and thoughts by means of indirect messages and behavioural impacts rather than direct verbal communication.[12] You will be probably be well aware of this from observing people at work. The office manager, for example, who stands in the kitchen, tutting loudly and asking, "Whose dirty mug is this?" or your colleague, who keeps getting up to answer the door buzzer, sighing gustily as he does so.

Communication styles

The idea of communication styles takes Ivanov's study and argues that the style you choose to use to communicate has as much impact as the words you use – that is, you choose your style to convey the message you want. This is important when we think about what can get in the way of good feedback.

Often, people choose a particular style to amplify their message, to convey how they feel, instead of clearly articulating the impact of the behaviour. When you find a message difficult to hear, sometimes this can also be a reaction to the style of communication as much as the message.

Ivanov identified four different types of communication behaviour:

1. aggressive
2. assertive
3. passive
4. passive aggressive.

Have a think about your own communication, and how it might get in the way when you give or receive feedback? Where does yours typically sit?

Aggressive

The aggressive style is the one you choose if you want to put someone in their place and give feedback in a way that puts them down. It's a style that assumes your rights are more important than those of others. This tends to be the style that sends people into flight or fight. In terms of the giving good feedback framework, it goes right to the core of the person. For example, comments like "not good enough", "you're useless", "you always", sarcasm, name calling, threatening, blaming, and being backward looking in feedback terms.

Passive

The passive style is one people often choose when they feel powerless. It is avoids saying "No" directly, and sometimes you say one thing to an employee and something else behind their back.

For example, "I don't mind having to redo all the PowerPoint slides. I just wonder if that's a good use of my time, but of course if you think it is, I'll put off the work I need to do for the board."

"Well, it's OK, there's just this tiny thing but I can see how you got that wrong. I mean I know it's hard to understand the idea behind a checklist."

Then you head off to a promotions meeting to talk about how useless they are, not able to do something as basic as follow a checklist, or the spelling mistakes you always have to correct in their presentations.

"Quiet quitting" could be described as a passive way of pointing out that you are feeling too overwhelmed to do your job, instead of having a conversation about the support you might need at work.[13] It is not helpful in feedback terms, because it isn't clear.

Passive aggressive

Passive aggressive brings the two together in the worst possible way. Witness that colleague who sighs gustily when answering the buzzer instead of suggesting employing a receptionist or taking turns. The manager who doesn't offer feedback to someone who hasn't completed a task but says, "Don't mind me, I'll do both our work shall I? I see you are struggling to keep up in this high-performance environment."

Assertive

The style that is most effective when giving feedback (and indeed when communicating clearly generally) is the assertive style.

This means you are confident enough to communicate what you need without resorting to manipulation or bullying. It achieves goals without hurting others and asserts your rights while acknowledging other people's.

"Stop it, I don't like it" is a good example, as long as you give a clear description of what the person is to stop doing and the negative impact it has on you, and then allow discussion about their take on the situation.

In feedback terms, an assertive communication style means you directly acknowledge the impact of the behaviour you see. It leaves you able to take it a step further – to discuss the other person's views and how you might move forward.

Putting communication styles to work

You may be overreliant on one particular communication style. Or you may also have an arsenal of different communication styles but default to a favourite when under stress. If your personal style of communication is not to be direct – for example, if you are used to your family skirting round issues – the first few times you receive direct feedback will be a shock.

If you are not used to receiving clear feedback, communicated politely and directly with no hint of meanness or aggression, this can be a hard skill to learn. But it remains a skill that can be learnt rather than an inherent trait. With the right sort of feedback from others, you can learn to adapt your communication style for different situations.

Noa, a graduate trainee, has been told she needs to improve her communication skills after feedback that staff consider her aggressive. It transpires that she is new to the job and is struggling with creating a rota and deciding how to move people around to ensure all breaks are covered.

She is slightly frightened of all the older women she is supposed to be managing. They all seem very experienced and set in their ways, and they all have specific times they like to go off for their coffee break. Noa decides she just has to let them know who is the boss. So at the morning meeting, she does exactly that.

"You, you and you," she barks at a couple of sales assistants. "You'll have to move to third break."

Then she walks off. One of the sales assistants, Jill, follows her.

"May I have a word, Noa," she says. "I want you to know that of course we will all change our breaks, if you ask us to. You're

91

the boss. However, I also want you to know, I really did not like the way you just asked me."

"Why?" says Noa (feeling extremely threatened and with no idea how she is supposed to assert her authority). "What was wrong with it?"

Jill sits down in the office with her and they discuss the feedback she has just offered to Noa. Jill's feedback is not aggressive or mean. She is not refusing to do what Noa has asked. She is simply clearly expressing her view about how that communication made her feel.

This is valuable learning for Noa. She hasn't previously been aware that when she is stressed and doesn't know how to solve a problem, she comes across as aggressive. She can now choose to develop some other ways of communicating and solving problems next time she feels like this.

She decides that the next time she has trouble covering breaks, she will make greater use of the women's experience, ask them how they will cover the rota and if they can agree any changes between themselves.

This is what she does. The outcome is the same, but the women feel in control and Noa feels less stressed. Both these things work in her favour the next time she needs them to put themselves out for the organisation.

Clarity and cultural background

Depending on the culture in which you live and work, there will be many accepted means of communicating. I once coached a client who regularly gave feedback known as "Rolf's revolving door feedback".

Rolf had joined a new organisation. He thought he had a

great, direct communication style and believed in giving very clear feedback, making sure his team knew where they stood. He also had what he called an "up or out policy". He thought it only fair to let members of staff who were not performing (not on their way up, as he saw it) know that their career was over. Then he expected them to leave.

"I showed them the door. They left. Sorted," he told his new colleagues confidently, after one conversation.

However, the member of staff came back into work happily the next day. Rolf didn't quite know how to challenge them or what to say. While he pondered, he gave the same message to a couple of other members of staff. They too came back into work the next day. This happened several times.

Eventually he came to ask for help. "I don't understand what's going on," he said.

It turned out that in Rolf's previous company "up or out" was the norm. Everyone was braced, all the time, for the feedback "You won't make partner here", closely followed by "Let's look and see if we can place you with a client." They understood the deal.

The bright young millennials at Rolf's new company had no experience of this sort of culture. They valued the idea of being given feedback in order to learn. Staff members knew they'd had a chat with Rolf and had got the vague message that he expected them to work a bit harder to progress. They weren't entirely sure that progression was really what they wanted, so hadn't given it a lot more thought.

Faced with this incomprehension, Rolf had spent a lot a time waffling. He had to learn to give clear, timely feedback that helped his team understand how he thought they were doing, in the job he needed them to do, right then and there. Deciding to leave or stay and improve was then up to them.

It is important to take time to understand how each individual that you work with communicates, as well as understanding your own preferred or habitual style. The style you use does not make you who you are; it is not an inherent personality trait. You can learn to use a range of communication styles for different purposes when the need arises – or if, like Noa, you get feedback that your particular style is not being received as you would wish.

Of course, you may not have a member of staff like Jill, willing to come forward and offer you supportive, helpful feedback. To learn more about yourself, and the way your behaviour is perceived, you will have to remember to ask for feedback in the first place.

Fortunately, you know a lot more about how to do that now. And, happily, there is more learning to come.

Remember

- Everyone carries their own baggage in the workplace.
- This can trip you up when you least expect it.
- Feedback can be useful, even if you find it difficult to hear.
- Explore your own baggage so that it does not get in the way.
- The stories you tell yourself will have an impact on how easy you find it to learn from feedback.
- You will also be influenced by your preferred communication styles, your cultural work experiences and your early experiences of feedback.

5

Bias

"We need no extra cunning, no new ideas, no unnecessary gadgets, no frantic hyperactivity – all we need is less irrationality."

Rolf Dobelli[1]

Once upon a time there was a keen young HR manager (Clinton) who was developing a new appraisal system. The system was competency based and had a five-point scale, with descriptions of the level of performance expected at each level. The idea was that managers could provide nuanced feedback, to match the scale. Clinton spent hours agreeing the different levels and competency wording with the teams and was pleased with himself. It was pretty sophisticated, if he said so himself (which of course he did, quite often). The only downside was that the system did not seem to be working. Pretty much everyone in the company was rated a 3. Every time.

After a frustrating ratings meeting, where no decisions about promotions could be made because of the similarity of the ratings (and after much grief and hand wringing on Clinton's part), the CEO decided the system had to change.

"We have to smash this middle-ranking tendency," he

said. "Force people into making a decision. Get some honest feedback going."

Dutifully, Clinton developed a new system with a different scale, a four-point scale this time, rating people from 1 to 4. This had new detailed competencies and descriptions of each level. Clinton spent many hours agreeing the wording of these new competencies, with a range of now rather bored teams across the organisation.

At ratings time, the CEO looked to see if there had been a change. And there had. Across the organisation, the ratings had changed. There were no more 3 rankings. Result. Or was it?

No, it wasn't. Everyone was now rated a 2/3. Still all average. A department full of average people? Surely "average" is a mathematical concept, not a real thing relating to actual people? An emergency consultant, drafted in to safeguard Clinton's sanity, explained to the CEO and Clinton that this was an example of a rating bias known as middle-ranking bias or centrality bias. The one Clinton's whole new system had been designed to smash.

Biases: what are they?

Let's think a bit more about bias and how they work.

Everyone has to make millions of decisions a day: what time do I have to get up, how should I travel to work, what shall I have for breakfast, should I get a new job, move house, have full cream, skimmed or almond milk in my latte? As the day goes on at work, you will have to decide what opinion you want to put forward about a new IT system, whether should you recruit a new receptionist or move Luna over from accounts, what feedback you should be giving to Jack, who still hasn't managed to complete three of the tasks you gave him last week.

The world is complex, so your brain helps you out by looking for patterns and associations and filtering out non-essential information. It has to, otherwise you would be overwhelmed. When under high levels of stress, your brain takes even more shortcuts. This is because people tend to use different parts of their brains when they are stressed than when they are relaxed and comfortably focused. When you are stressed, you do not think properly. Rules of thumb, educated guesses and using common sense are all forms of mental shortcuts. Implicit or unconscious bias is a result of taking one of these cognitive shortcuts as you incorrectly rely on unconscious stereotypes to provide guidance in a very complex world.[2] Under high levels of stress, you are more likely to rely on these biases than to examine all the relevant, surrounding information.[3]

Unconscious bias

While Clinton was struggling to create the perfect, unbiased rating system, one of the managers, Charlie, was trying to give feedback to his team managers. He was confused by the whole rating scheme but didn't worry too much about it. He always rated in the middle to be on the safe side, like the rest of the organisation. Basically, his two managers, Sarah and Alan, were fine except they both seemed to have issues dealing with clients. Sarah, normally quite feisty, seemed to close down and go very quiet when she met a client. Charlie noted on her feedback form, "She seems to go into herself when she talks to clients, shows no personality and should be more confident. Promotion is some way off."

Alan was also not getting the results expected. Like Sarah, he did not seem to get on particularly well with clients. However, Charlie had high hopes for Alan. He had handpicked Alan because they had gone to the same school and had the same sort of approach to work. Charlie was sure that Alan had the necessary skills and potential; he probably just needed some more practice. Sarah, however, had been foisted on Charlie by another department, after she came back from maternity leave last month. So, on Alan's feedback form, Charlie noted, "Alan will develop his undoubted customer service skills with more exposure. Recommend promotion to encourage this development."

Charlie was summoned to the HR department to discuss his comments. Along with the efforts to smash the middle-ranking tendency, the CEO also wanted to encourage people to discuss ratings they were not happy with. Sarah was not happy with her feedback. Clinton, as HR manager, was following up.

Charlie was shocked to be asked to defend his feedback. He didn't think he was being less generous to Sarah just because she was a woman. She just wasn't as able. Well, all right she had the same rating as Alan, but that was just the way the ratings worked, wasn't it? And he did think Alan had more potential. He was not entirely sure why, he just did.

Bingo! Here are at least four biases, demonstrated all in one go.

Of course, Clinton did not say "Bingo!" Apart from anything else, he was too worn down by the tedious comments from the consultant and irrational requests from the CEO to make any kind of joke.

But he did draw attention to all these four biases

(idiosyncratic rater bias, attribution bias, similar-to-me bias and confirmation bias) and he recommended that Charlie went on an unconscious bias course. Charlie was shaken at the idea of being in any way biased or prejudiced, and wandered off to his course in a daze.

Do you have any affinity with Charlie? How much awareness do you think you have of your biases? Do they impact on the way you give feedback to your team?

Before you think too hard about this, I should warn you, this is a trick question. Whatever your answer is, you will probably be wrong. This is because many biases are unconscious. By definition, therefore, like Charlie, you are just not aware of them.

Studies show that unconscious bias courses by themselves are not the answer. Awareness of unconscious bias can lead to people to suppress comments that they know display their bias.[4] However, without further support (and careful feedback on their behaviour and how they are displaying bias) they still retain the bias and the behaviour that goes with it. What's more, there can then be a reaction, leading to worse behaviour than before.

As Charlie insightfully commented at the end of his course, "It's a bit like playing Whack-a-mole. I find out about one bias, try to do something about it and another one just pops up to take its place."

Giving good feedback requires you to know yourself, so that you can explore ways of negating these biases. Then you are less likely to fall into a bias trap or be tripped up by a deeply buried bias when you are trying to offer forward-looking, developmental feedback.

The starting point is to explore a bit more about what is going on for you. In the first place, you might reasonably ask how you are supposed to work out what your biases are if you can't see them.

Surface your unconscious bias

You may think that if you look hard enough at something, you will see all there is to see. However, there will be times when you won't notice something, even when you are looking right at it. Magic, for example, works by exploiting our collective cognitive biases, or blind spots and unawareness of our mind's limitations.

But magicians don't change what you can see – they will simply manipulate your false beliefs about what you **think** you can see. This isn't because you aren't looking at the right place; your mind is simply misdirected.

This tendency has important practical implications in daily life. It is dangerous for example, to drive while talking on a mobile phone. Even though you are looking at the cars in front of you, the phone conversation distracts your attention. And it is this mental distraction, or misdirection, that prevents you from noticing the oncoming car, even though you might be looking straight at it.

You face the same tendency when you are trying to give good feedback and avoid bias at work. There will be a variety of factors that have influenced your mind and so your cognition. The feedback you give will always reflect these influences. Sometimes this can mean that your feedback is misdirected. On these occasions, it reflects these influences and biases more than the behaviour of the person you are giving feedback to.

It will have the same effect as a car, completely outside your consciousness, driving straight at you. The best outcome you can hope for is to crash into HR, like Charlie, preferably before anyone sues you for discrimination.

Where do all these influences come from?

Social and cultural influences

Influences from media, culture and your upbringing will contribute to the implicit associations you form about the members of social groups and will ingrain specific biases in your mind.

For example, the way TV portrays individuals can lead people to associate particular cultural groups with criminals or think that particular professions are the exclusive preserve of men or women. Parental attitudes, siblings, the school setting and the culture in which children grow up can also influence implicit prejudice. As anyone who has spent time in a playground will recognise, children notice not just the similarities and differences but also that the children who are different in some way to the largest group, have a hard time. This can ingrain the thought that "what is similar to me is good, and what is different from me is bad".[5]

The biases you hold as a result of this conditioning can then be the source of unfairness and lack of inclusivity at work. They will also affect the things you give feedback about, the way you give feedback and even who you are prepared to give feedback to.[6] Charlie, in our example earlier would not have described himself as biased against women. He would have balked at the idea that he gave Alan a job just because he went to the same school and defended to the death the idea that Alan was a much better salesperson than Sarah. But he was still incapable of giving unbiased feedback.

So, one question to ask yourself as you prepare to give feedback, in order to surface any bias, is, "Am I really giving feedback? Or am I really saying, "Why can't you be more like me?"

Let's explore some different biases.

Feedback-blighting biases

Once you start looking at different biases, it can be hard to know when to stop, or even where to focus, as you start improving yourself. So here are four key biases that you can begin to look out for when you are thinking about feedback.

Confirmation bias

This bias works like this. You make a decision or form an opinion, like Charlie comparing his two members of staff. ("Alan is a good chap, I went to school with him; this Sarah woman has just been foisted on me by Clinton, no one else wants her.")

Then you look for, and value, any further information that confirms your opinion. You could also think of confirmation bias as cherry picking or wishful thinking. This means that, like Charlie, you end up interpreting things in a certain way or ignoring other information that contradicts your initial thinking.

Charlie is biased towards Alan. He expects him to be good at his job, because he thinks Alan is like him. Everywhere he looks he sees plenty of confirming evidence, while indications to the contrary remain unseen or are quickly dismissed as exceptions or special cases. For example, it is quite clear that Alan is not good with customers. However Charlie still hangs on to his opinion that he will magically improve with more experience. He has become blind to evidence to the contrary.

The halo and horns effect

This builds on confirmation bias. It occurs when one perceived positive feature or trait makes us view everything about a person in a positive way, giving them a "halo". But we may not know much about the person, and the halo effect can lead us to ignore other aspects.

You can also see this effect when it comes to deciding how to reward people for their work. The Nobel laureate Herbert Simon, social scientist and one of the founding fathers of artificial intelligence, believed that once you win one award and become well known, your name is much more likely to surface when an award committee gets together. This can also happen in organisations, when promotions rest on decisions made by senior managers who have only the haziest knowledge of a team member's work.

Charlie's feedback on Alan's performance is flawed and based on his confirmation bias towards Alan. Alan, however, has had the good fortune to make one sale at the beginning of the year. This was a complete fluke, achieved largely as a result of Sarah's background work with the customer, something Charlie ignored. The fact that Alan has made no sales since then does not matter; the senior manager at the promotions meeting remembers the original sale, because Alan reminds him about it every time they meet at the coffee machine. So the senior manager happily signs off Charlie's recommendation of promotion for Alan.

The horn effect works in the same sort of way, but for opposite reasons, so we focus on one particularly negative feature (Sarah is quiet with customers) and don't offer any other opportunities or rewards for that person.

Attribution bias

In social psychology, attribution is the process of inferring the causes of events or behaviours. In real life, attribution is something we all do every day, usually without being aware of the underlying processes and biases that lead to our inferences.

When it comes to other people, we tend to attribute causes to internal factors such as personality characteristics and ignore or minimise external variables. Psychologists refer to this tendency as the fundamental attribution error. Even though situational variables are very likely present, we automatically attribute the cause to personal characteristics.

If, for example, someone is late for a meeting, you extrapolate something totally disconnected from this. (Batu hasn't turned up on time twice in a row, therefore he is lazy.) Over the course of a typical day, you probably make numerous attributions like this about the people around you.

Take a minute to consider the impact your attribution errors may have on the way you think about other people. Batu is always late, therefore he is lazy; Carlotta is not committed to the job, because she is not keeping up with her work. Alan is generally splendid, a great salesperson, because he tells me about his sales at the coffee machine.

Do these attributions make sense? Have you discussed with Batu what happened to make him late today? Why do you think Carlotta is not committed? What does not keeping up with her work mean? What did you see her do or not do? Have you noticed that Alan spends most of his morning at the coffee machine, and tells you about the same sale every time you meet?

When you are considering your own tendencies in this regard, it may help you to be aware that when it comes to explaining our own behaviour, people tend to have the opposite bias. When something negative happens to us, we are more likely to blame external forces than our personal characteristics. In psychology, this tendency is known as the actor–observer bias or self-serving theory.

So, if you are late for the same meeting as Batu, you know this is definitely *not* because you are lazy. You know you are fanatically committed to your job. However, you also have many domestic responsibilities. You work hard to make sure your children are safely off to school and also have to wait for your aged mother's carer to arrive before you leave the house. You cannot help it if your children are lazy and make you late by sleeping in, and the carer is disorganised, always arriving after the specified time.

This theory highlights the importance of being able to discuss any feedback (based on behaviour you have observed) with the people concerned. Otherwise, the fact that Batu has a new baby or Carlotta is now managing twice as many outlets as this time last year and has had trouble recruiting new staff, may be conveniently glossed over in your head. Always ask for the other person's side of the story when giving good feedback.

Data and idiosyncratic rater bias

Part of the reason that bias can get in the way of giving good feedback is a flawed understanding about data and the way it works. If you make decisions (or offer feedback) using the data you have drawn from your head, this will be flawed. In other words, when you try to do this, you will face something any self-respecting data analyst would call "data insufficiency".

On what basis was Charlie making a decision about rating his people on the new system? What data are you using to decide on Suella's ability to "synthesise situations" or Rolf's ability to "fight to get in synch" or even Christophe's "conceptual thinking?"

These are some of the descriptions that Ray Dalio used to provide real-time feedback as part of his radical transparency approach. His view was that having a lot of people providing rating data at the same time made the rating data (and therefore the resulting feedback) better.

An opposing view is that our in-built biases become magnified when lots of ratings are put together. Rather like a river, fed by tributary streams, approaching a downhill slope. A lot of individually flawed opinions, influenced by our unconscious bias, simply become a lot of flawed opinions, all aggregated to make one gigantic, river of flawed opinion, leading to a waterfall of unhelpful feedback.[7]

You can see this demonstrated in any competition, from the Olympics to the first prize for the biggest vegetable in a country show. Surely it should be easy enough to decide which marrow is biggest? How many variables can there be? Not many, you might think, compared with the range of points you have to hold in your mind when considering a rating for "business acumen" or "conceptual thinking".

But even so, judging panels in country shows can struggle to agree, argue furiously and end up with an incomprehensible decision, based on flawed data. Why is it flawed? There are careful definitions of what "large marrow" means.

The decision is flawed because it will come laced with a liberal sprinkling of all the different biases, prejudices and feelings of the judging panel. These will be about both the vegetables and the different vegetable growers, plus the individual experiences, cultural backgrounds and preferences of the panel. Once these are aggregated, it ensures an apparently irrational decision. Then no one is happy with the outcome, potentially leading to deep and long-held resentments.[8]

In the same way, rating at work according to a competency model will have far more to do with each rater's personality and experience than the competency model itself.[9] So aggregating them has the same effect.

Recommendations for overcoming bias

You may be wondering what you are supposed to do about all this. You may understand different bias, but still struggle with exactly how you are supposed to get this data or information about your bias when, by definition, unconscious biases are unconscious? How can you become aware of something buried so deep within your consciousness? Of course, education and training can help with recognising these biases. Unconscious bias training, cultural awareness courses and online tests (such as implicit attitude tests) are methods employed to do this.[10] Many organisations also run cultural awareness training to learn, for example, about other cultures or outgroups and what language and behaviours they may find offensive.[11]

The jury is still out on how useful these are.[12] And as we know, simply raising awareness of bias is not enough.

So how can you go about changing your behaviour at work to make sure it is not biased? How can you get yourself some helpful data about the way all those unconscious things impact on your behaviour. How can you begin to understand the difference between your intentions (the impact you mean to have) and what other people notice (the impact your behaviour actually has on others)?

That's right! Ask for some feedback.

Feedback gives us valuable data about the way we come across to others. It helps us identify the gap between what we *intend* and what *actually happens* when we are interacting with other people. Once you have this information, you can discuss and decide what you want to do about it.

You can review your own feedback fallacies by making a checklist of things you need to look out for to avoid bias. Then you can start to think about altering the behaviours that previously meant you gave biased feedback. You will probably find you can adjust five points quite easily.

- Avoid the "recency effect" leading to halo and horns bias by having regular feedback discussions.
- Keep track of these discussions and any information or data you are using to make a judgement and that you might use to make a judgement in the future. Look for themes and trends, rather than jumping on a one-off piece of behaviour that you like or don't like. This will help you build up data that is free of idiosyncratic rater bias.

- Interrogate the data you have gathered. Talk to your subconscious, or review your subconscious thoughts, articulating them out loud, with a colleague, preferably with a very different background to you. This will help you identify any similar-to-me tendencies and bring your confirmation bias to the surface.

- Ask a colleague (again, preferably one with a different background to yours) to "check" you when you are making decisions or carrying out activities that might display bias, such as promotion decisions and recruitment. You may think you display no bias; they may see things differently.

- Remember that there is a reason why cultures around the world teach important life lessons and values through fables, fairy tales and myths. People like stories. They are more memorable than disjointed facts. Examine the narratives you create around people. Examine the narratives you build around yourself. Review and compare the two. This will help you avoid some of the worse attribution errors.

By doing all this, you will be able to move round the learning circle and be able to implement a change.

Stress, perception and bias

Another point to consider is the effect of stress on your behaviour. When you are stressed, this is when your bias is likely to come to the fore, as your brain take shortcuts. The more you can be aware of this and the more you can decrease your stress, the more you can decrease a tendency to give feedback overly influenced by bias.

Some organisations are beginning to wake up to this, looking at the impact of stress on employees and setting up wellbeing initiatives to support them. You may be able to take advantage of these, or suggest them to your employer if they are not already available.

In the meantime, take a few minutes to consider your stress behaviours. Ask people you trust to give you feedback on what is different about the way you behave when you are under stress. Consider what you can do to change these behaviours, so that they do not trip you up. Then, when you know you have to give feedback, create some headspace for yourself. Practise something like mindfulness or mediation, use an app such as CALM, or simply take the initiative to block out space in your diary. This can give you the time and space you need to reduce the stress and decrease the pressure on your brain.[13]

If you are in the middle of a stressful situation, this is probably not the time to give feedback. By all means, make notes about what you notice, or file your observations away in your mind. But then wait a bit, so that you have time to interrogate your data before giving the feedback. This will leave you more open to giving feedback that is not laced with bias. (There are some worksheets in Part 3 to help with this.)

Lollapalooza bias and labels

The last of our five feedback blighting biases is this one, described colourfully by Charlie Munger as "lollapalooza" bias.[14]

This is demonstrated most clearly when a combination of cultural expectations around behaviour and organisational rating requirements come together, creating a perfect (nonsensical) storm.

The four horsemen were an example of this. The only feedback they enthusiastically embraced was feedback on the dress code, specifically the importance of black rather than brown shoes. Keen and inquisitive staff who produced a list of questions gathered on their first day were brushed aside with the comment, "Good to have you. Buy a pair of black shoes for tomorrow though, will you? Dress code. See you in the morning."

Staff who did not appreciate the significance of this feedback and rush to take it on board (or possibly could not afford new shoes) were ascribed as having "difficult" behaviour, despite being useful staff, in terms of their skills and knowledge.

Organisations who instead accept people as "spiky" and work to make the most of their strengths are like gold dust.[15] Going back to our earlier example, the job that Priya went back to was less well paid and less career-oriented than her new one. But her manager there knew how to look after her staff and make them feel appreciated.

She did that by focusing on their strengths and organising the team around them. Those with a customer focus were brought forward to share their knowledge, those with creative flair were given the window displays, those with an admin bent were involved in the office. Gradually people took on specialities. They all had to work as a team and do the bits they weren't so good at sometimes. But they all wanted to please the manager and do well, so they tried hard. The fame of the retail establishment she ran spread far and wide; people made special trips to meet the knowledgeable lovely staff. Over time, the competition to go and work there became huge.

The labels the horsemen applied, however, seeped back to

other things and hey presto, the person labelled as "difficult" became seen as generally useless. Often, this was a terrible waste: skills were not used and developed, people did not get feedback to help them learn, people who had all the right skills did not feel appreciated and so moved elsewhere.

This kind of labelling offers its own special type of bias.

Labels and bias

Even if you do not work in a large organisation with specific expectations of dress or behaviour, many people love a label. And as we tend to think like consumers, it is worth turning briefly to consumer research to think about labels and the impact they have on feedback.

According to research, one-third of product decision making is based on packaging alone. In the mind of a consumer, product packaging and product quality are directly related. A product with strong branding and packaging isn't just more likely to grab a customer's attention – it's also associated with high quality ingredients or contents.

A definition of the term "label" in consumer terms will reference three different types.

1. **brand label**: giving information about the brand
2. **descriptive label**: specifying product use
3. **grade label**: describing aspects and features of the product.

Advertisers know how important labels are and this is why so much is spent on brand awareness.

Pretty much the same thing happens at work.

Labelling is rife in organisations and this can seep into the sort of feedback you are likely to give. There will be people who you have decided have definite "brand" (Natacha – superstar; Den – arrogant idiot) so you give them suitable descriptive labels (this is Natacha – superstar, give her anything; Den – useless, avoid, except for unimportant projects) and, if you are pushed, a grade label (Natacha great at organisation; Den messes up everything).

This all starts way before we get to work, of course. Schools and families are prone to labelling too. Throughout your life, people will attach labels to you, and those labels reflect and affect how others think about your identity, as well as how you think about yourself. Take a minute to think about this, and note down any labels that you know are attached to you.

Labels are not always negative; they can also reflect positive characteristics and set useful expectations. Sometimes, they may even provide meaningful goals in your life. However, labels are associated with concepts such as self-fulfilling prophecy and stereotyping, which takes us straight back to bias.[16]

Labelling will have an impact on both Natacha and Den's behaviour. In fact, the labels that Natacha and Den are given at work will have an impact on how they learn at work and the type of work they get involved with. Over time this label will stick to pretty much everything they do. Natacha will get many more opportunities than Den. Den will struggle on, along with others who may also have been labelled as "useless", or as "plodders" or "reliable workhorses".

Of course, it may be that Den, Natacha and everyone in your organisation do indeed behave as they are labelled some of the time, even a lot of the time. The entire organisation may agree with you about the aptness of the label you have collectively bestowed upon them.

But the labels are not going to help them change their behaviour. This is because labels do not help you articulate what the impact of that behaviour is on you, the team or on the work you all need to produce. This applies to the great people as well as the less great ones. Natacha will not know what it is about her behaviour that is so great and so she will not know how much you and the organisation value it, or that you want to see more of it.

All she knows is that she is being given an awful lot more work than Den and this seems unfair. In fact, any minute now she is probably going to claim that you give the worst work to the women in the team, resign and go somewhere else where she might feel more appreciated, after threatening you with a discrimination claim.

So at the end of this chapter, you have two specific things to work on. One is to consider your bias and take steps to address it before giving feedback. The other is to seek feedback for yourself about the effect that your unconscious bias has on your behaviour. Once you have a structure in place for these two things, you will be further on your way towards giving good feedback.

Remember

- We are all subject to bias.
- The first step in overcoming our biases is to become more aware of them.
- The next step is to try and mitigate against common biases.
- We can do this by seeking feedback.
- Once we have the feedback, we can move round the learning circle.

6

Organisational culture

"No passion so effectually robs the mind of all its powers of acting and reasoning as *fear*."

Edmund Burke[1]

One of the managing partners at the four horsemen's organisation was an intelligent and well-meaning individual. He was well aware that to remain competitive and attract the brightest and the best recruits, the organisation had to change its approach. He led a culture change programme, emphasising the importance of values-based leadership, and he replaced the ratings/promotion meetings with a new appraisal system. The emphasis was on clear helpful, developmental, face-to-face feedback through regular feedback conversations.

This attracted a new generation of employees who were more interested in clear values, learning and development and work–life balance than in savaging their way to the top. For many of the new recruits, the idea of the appraisal scheme was exciting and developmental.

But managers were used to equating the idea of feedback with attributing blame and pointing out mistakes. They found the idea of offering developmental face-to-face feedback, encouraging people to learn, impossibly daunting. So they avoided all the training sessions on the new appraisal system and how to give good feedback. They put off holding any conversations about feedback or providing any written feedback at all. Consequently, at promotion meeting time, there were no ratings to look at. Without this data, the senior managers had no idea what to do.

They got an HR consultancy to devise a way that feedback could be sent and collated via a technology-based performance management system so that the data problem did not happen again. With a collective sigh of relief, all the managers stopped bothering with the face-to-face part and just sent the feedback via the system. This negated the idea of trying to improve the quality of feedback conversations.

Staff who had had what they thought were honest, developmental discussions found themselves marked down at promotion time. Key staff felt they had been misled about the organisation's values. The new generation of employees left to seek employment elsewhere, never to return. Profits dipped. The managing partner was replaced.

Learning and fear

Remember: the key purpose of good feedback is learning. However, it is not always easy to facilitate learning for others or to learn ourselves.

This is because the biggest single factor that gets in the way of learning is fear.

As we interact with other people, we are all trying to control what they think of us, both consciously and subconsciously. People therefore learn early on to avoid the risk of looking ignorant, incompetent or disruptive. Sociologist Erving Goffman comments on this, pointing out that although humans want to learn, they also remain inherently fearful when trying to join a group.[2]

It starts at school. I was always the child arriving at school with the overly large jumper, with holes in it, handed down from several sisters. It was no fun. What about you? Were you the child arriving in fancy dress clothes on the wrong day, the child without the homework, or the child everyone stared at because you didn't know the answer? Did the teachers help you out in those situations?

The culture of the school, and of individual teachers, has an impact on how safe children feel and how easily they learn.

Learning gets even harder as an adult, in the workplace, where most people feel they are being paid to know what to do and so are even more afraid of looking foolish. Have you ever woken up in the morning thinking, "Who do I want to be today? I know, the one person in the meeting who can't remember the goals, hasn't brought the right agenda, and is wearing the wrong sort of clothes?"

Unlikely.

Most people just want to get on and do their best. If there are things you need to learn to do your job better, the likelihood is that you probably want to learn them. But just how much your work environment helps or hinders you when you try to learn, and therefore how open you are to feedback, will depend on many factors. The environment you are in influences and can reinforce or mitigate different behaviours.

Psychological safety

There is growing evidence that people can only learn well and benefit from feedback if they feel psychologically safe at work.[3] But what does this mean in organisational terms?

If you work on an oil rig, for example, you may be working in physically dangerous conditions, regularly undertaking dangerous diving expeditions. However, if you have confidence that all the safety procedures are followed, your team regularly discuss issues and problems, you work together to continually minimise risk and you feel that your team leader has your back, then you probably feel psychologically safe.

Or you could work in a warm comfortable office, with no apparent physical hazards in sight. Your working conditions are physically perfectly safe.

But if the team meetings involve finding scapegoats and humiliating them and everyone sits quivering at their desks, waiting to be shouted at for something they didn't do, you will not feel safe at all.

You also would not dream of going diving with your team, because everyone would have covered up all the mistakes and it would be terribly dangerous, physically. It would be almost as bad as that corporate away day, when you were supposed to trust Colin from Accounts to catch you, if you fell backwards with your eyes shut.

This is because there are different kinds of safety; the safety lacking in the second example is psychological safety. This is the kind of safety Amy Edmondson explores in her book *The Fearless Organisation*.

Organisations today benefit enormously from effective teamwork, with employees spending 50% more time collaborating than they did twenty years ago.[4] Many organisations have multidisciplinary teams all over the world. And, to work effectively as a team, we all need to be able to give and receive good feedback. Research about psychological safety therefore raises many important points to consider when thinking of organisational culture, feedback and working well with colleagues. Chief among them is that building psychological safety in an organisation means creating the right conditions for feedback and supporting people to move into a learning mindset.

Edmondson points out that this is not a new concept. Back in the 1960s, for example, Edgar Schein and Warren Bennis looked at the impact that organisational change can have on employees' ability to hear feedback and to learn.[5] Schein pointed out that psychological safety was important in order to overcome the learning anxiety and defensiveness that people demonstrate, especially when something doesn't go to plan. This safety, he said, allows people to focus on shared goals rather than on self-protection.

So, in a psychologically safe workplace, people are more likely to feel comfortable with a concept like compassionate candour and the interpersonal risks that involves. They don't worry as much about sharing their ideas or try and second guess what more senior people think. They are too busy participating enthusiastically. This leads to an environment where helpful feedback can be shared, mistakes are tackled quickly, and teams coordinate across departments to create good systems. People talk about bringing their full selves to work and seek feedback on how they can achieve their personal best.

Of course, this utopian ideal is not easy to create. If you work in an organisation where appraisal systems are based on scores rather than timely discussion of development, you are more likely to spend time wondering what you have to do to make sure you get the best grade and therefore a higher promotion than Kevin from the Paris office than meditating on how you can bring your best and full self to work.

Communication styles and cultural differences

What about the way you communicate within your organisation? How might you need to adapt your behaviour so that you communicate feedback in a way that makes all your team feel psychologically safe enough to learn from it?

This is always important, but particularly so if you work globally. Different cultures can vary in how direct they are in communication and how they approach communicating feedback. As a result, people who are in the same team but in different corners of the globe may have entirely different experiences of how safe they feel when receiving feedback.

It is easy to reduce this dynamic to cultural stereotypes, and this is not a book on cultural awareness. However, the way your team feels about the feedback they receive at work will depend, in part, on the style of communication they are culturally used to.

They may, for example, be based in the Netherlands but be receiving feedback from a manager in France and giving feedback to someone in Japan. All these countries may have different cultures and different communication style norms. In the Netherlands, the norm can be for people to give very direct feedback. Arguing or debating an intellectual concept vigorously with a manager is considered absolutely fine in France but is definitely not a concept understood in Japan.

This can all take a bit of practice and getting used to. When talking to engineers in Japan, Brian, our example from earlier, had to get used to asking oblique questions about the accuracy of data. He could never simply point out that it was wrong. He knew when he asked questions and the engineers said, "Nothing wrong, nothing wrong, boss," they would run straight off after the conversation to put right whatever he had raised in his questions. He got the feedback he needed to adapt his own communication style (obliquely) by paying careful attention to their behaviour. As a result, the work that the engineers needed to do was completed correctly.

Hierarchy and leadership styles

When it comes to giving the right message about the importance of psychologically safe, positive feedback cultures, it's also critically important for leaders to walk the talk, showing themselves as being open to feedback.

Leaders who are constantly seeking, inviting and (most importantly) *acting on* feedback can encourage an open culture in the organisation. If everyone is constantly asking, "What do you think? What could I change? How could I improve this?", feedback can become part of the everyday corporate dialogue.

However, people need to feel psychologically safe enough to do this. The culture in Silicon Valley, the home of radical candour, was one where the top leaders would relish being shouted down by others via direct feedback. However, as we have discussed, shouting down and offering direct feedback that is not respectful or polite is not the same as offering helpful feedback.

How do you get the balance right and make sure that the way you give feedback to someone in Japan is not threatening, but make it direct enough for someone in the United States to take on board?

Useful leadership styles

A good starting point is to look at leadership styles and the impact these can have on psychological safety within organisations.

The four horsemen led via a culture of fear. When things got very difficult for them, just before the company collapsed, they tried to suggest that this was due to a few bad apples who didn't know how to behave. Frantic efforts made by Belinda (and many others) to shred incriminating documents possibly suggested otherwise.

However, if you traced the problems back, the root cause for the difficulties was the leadership throughout the organisation. There was a right way to behave and a wrong way to behave. If you chose to behave in the wrong way, you didn't last long. If mistakes were discovered, a scapegoat was found rather than a solution. Bits were regularly chipped off people through critical feedback to help people learn how to fit the corporate mould. No one questioned this leadership approach. Everyone was too afraid. The best way to avoid damaging feedback was to throw it at someone else first.

Amy Edmondson contends that while everyone has a role to play to create a psychologically safe culture and a work environment that supports learning, leaders have a special contribution to make. It is worth considering the traits that can be most useful.[6]

Research into different styles of leadership and the impact these can have on a team suggests that there is no one bad style (such as obnoxious aggression) that must be avoided at all costs.[7] However, these are *styles*, not fixed traits, and leaders will need to use a mixture of them, depending on the stage of the organisation.

- Coercive leaders demand immediate compliance.
- Authoritative leaders mobilise people towards a vision.
- Affiliative leaders create emotional bonds and harmony.
- Democratic leaders build consensus through participation.
- Pacesetting leaders expect excellence and self-direction.
- Coaching leaders develop people for the future.

Flexibility and the emotional intelligence to move around leadership styles as required is crucial if teams are to feel psychologically safe. A leader's emotional intelligence creates a certain culture or work environment and is critical to psychological safety.[8]

High levels of emotional intelligence support the creation of a culture where information sharing, trust, healthy risk-taking and learning flourish. Low levels of emotional intelligence, however, tend to create climates beset with fear and anxiety.

Humility

The importance of humility in leaders and the ability to ask questions has led to a more recent trend – that of "don't knowing", which celebrates leaders asking for feedback on their leadership, in a humble and more gentle way than the Silicon Valley approach.[9]

I coach many enthusiastic and lovely CEOs of small businesses who have taken this approach to heart and are thoroughly committed to learning the newest leadership techniques. One CEO wanted to improve the feedback-giving skills in his team and encourage everyone to bring their full selves to work. He had read Kim Scott's book *Radical Candor* and wanted to implement it in full.

He had just recovered from mourning the lack of interest from his team in BHAGs (big hairy audacious goals). The team were quite happy with their current goals, set earlier that month. In fact, they developed their own new phrase for the CEO: SSH goals (sensible, suitable, happy goals).

His bid to introduce radical candour was meeting the same sort of resistance. Feedback from his team, after watching a training video, suggested they were not fully on board. In the video, the perennially enthusiastic Kim Scott and her colleagues take turns to shout the key message of the radical candour approach. "Say what you think. Say what you think. Just say what you think! Say it!"

"What *exactly* are we supposed to be saying, though?" queried one team member. "I really don't like this approach. It scares me."

Helping people feel safe to learn

Giving good feedback starts with a culture where people feel safe enough to learn. And building good relationships between team members is key to this. How you do this depends partly on size. If you set up a small dotcom with a schoolfriend, perhaps the care and the relationships you have with each other can be taken for granted.

However, as a start-up begins to grow, relationships do not scale. You cannot spend your day "just saying it" with people you barely know. Some organisations try to overcome this by having open emailing policies, where every email you send appears in the inbox of every employee in the company, to avoid subconscious office politics.

But building a psychologically safe workspace, where people feel able to offer each other good feedback, does not necessarily require systems like this. The trick is to find a way of creating an honest, open culture, an environment of trust where people can learn. As discussed earlier, one of the most effective ways to do that is for leaders to seek feedback and act on it themselves.

The CEO mentioned above had the best of intentions. He wanted his team to be able to give good feedback. Reluctantly, he began to understand that running in with new initiatives for his team every month did not make people feel psychologically safe. He tried out "don't knowing" and asked people to give him feedback on his approach.

He listened to people's feedback, detailing their concerns about his ideas for introducing radical candour techniques. It wasn't that they were not interested in giving good feedback; they were perfectly willing to explore and consider different approaches. However, they did not want to rush into something that did not feel quite right, culturally, for them all at that time. The CEO needed to start more slowly.

He compromised by introducing a few techniques relating specifically to positive feedback at team meetings (keeping a "Ta-dah!" list as well as a to-do list and sharing your best "Ta-dah!" success moments from the week, for example). He built up the organisation's ability to give and receive good feedback from there.

In doing this, he modelled another important point for leaders who aim to create a culture of psychological safety and feedback: they have to be open to feedback, and really listen to it. Most importantly, they need to be seen to be prepared to discuss and act on feedback. If they don't, why would anyone else bother?

There are a range of interventions and processes that can signal your willingness to learn as an organisation.

In the modern, psychologically safe workplace, teamwork and collaboration are more important than top-down, command-and-control leadership. Rather than confidential upward feedback for example, or 360 feedback systems that anonymise feedback, it is useful to share and learn from feedback as a team.

Kim Scott proffers a process called "Whoops a Daisy". This involves getting people – managers and leaders included – to stand up in a meeting and share a story about a mistake they have made that week. Everyone involved needs to know that they get instant and automatic forgiveness for the mistake they share. This, she comments, gets people comfortable with sharing their mistakes and is extremely valuable for creating a culture of feedback and learning. The person with the best story wins the stuffed Daisy Duck toy.

Whatever technique you choose, these models help more junior colleagues feel more comfortable with discussing learning, through both successes and mistakes. As a result, they see more senior people as human beings, learning and growing too.

Corporate stories

In the four horsemen's company, it was a badge of honour for people to dread your feedback. "Everyone hates working for me. I always pick up their spelling mistakes," recounted one manager happily.

In another organisation, great pleasure was taken in recounting to new staff members the time Ashley forgot to enter the runners for the London Marathon. "We lost out on hundreds of pounds," the office manager would say gleefully.

In contrast, the CEO mentioned earlier would personally introduce new recruits to the team, explaining each person's roles and responsibilities and describing them with variations on adjectives like "brilliant" or "amazing". He would follow this up with an example of what fantastic support the new recruit could go to that person for.

Consider the stories that you share in your organisation. Are they about those times when someone forgot to do something? Hideous crises involving lots of blame? Or are they about successes? Do you take joy in recognising talent? Are you giving feedback because you look at what people do well and enjoy pointing that out? Or do you love nit picking and finding fault? Pecking them like chickens, as Margaret Heffernan would say.

Good feedback will always be forward looking, focusing on what people can learn. Apportioning blame is never a helpful organisational culture. In the four horsemen's organisation, everyone spent too much time working out who to blame, who to chip a bit off to deflect attention from themselves. Over time, everyone was too busy looking out for their jobs either to offer or learn from helpful feedback.

Clarity

Sometimes managers have trouble giving feedback about performance because they are not clear about what the employee is supposed to be doing. In cultures of fear, people are often afraid, simply because they don't know quite what they are supposed to be doing, and they have always been too afraid to ask. They may have long job descriptions that include requirements for skills they will never be able to develop and which make no sense. But they don't want to admit this, because the culture does not support learning. In fact, it probably ridicules anyone who asks questions.

Because of this, managers are more likely to become aggressive when challenged or babble a lot of jargon to cover themselves. Unhelpful, damaging feedback that makes people afraid to ask for more, is much easier and carries much less risk (for the boss.) People then just go off and sit quietly at their desks, ducking every time they see the boss coming near.

Psychological safety, and therefore the ability to hear feedback, needs to start with clarity around expectations.

To make sure your corporate culture supports learning and giving good feedback, map out:

- **what** is expected of people in a role (break it down into actions and behaviours)

Then give managers the skills to point out:

- **when** it is being done, or
- **when** it is **not** being done.

Then emphasise the importance of explaining:

- **how** it is being done, or
- **how** it **is not** being done.

Build into this the explicit expectation that time should be spent pointing out when people have done things well. This is as valuable to learning as pointing out when things have gone wrong. Arguably, focusing on the things you do well simply means that you are reaping a reward sooner, targeting your efforts where you will get most return.[10] It just makes it a smaller hill to climb.

The key to this is the discussion you hold when you give feedback. People can feel safe with almost any feedback, as long as it is focused on something they can do something about (i.e. behaviour) and it is discussed in detail, with the opportunity to put forward their own view.

Unfortunately, organisational expectations of appraisals and ratings tend to encourage people to equate giving feedback with formal processes or systems held once or twice a year. Even when organisations perceive the limitations of Feedback with a capital F, popular feedback models, if misunderstood or misinterpreted, can confuse rather than clarify about why feedback is being given and what the recipient is being asked to do or change as a result.

For example, Pendleton's rules are a well-established way of giving feedback designed to help feedback givers involve the other person in the conversation. The idea is that they should first look at what has gone well and then at what could be done better. Figure 4 on the next page gives the steps in a feedback conversation that follows Pendleton's rules.

Unfortunately, the interpretation of feedback conversations in many workplaces has led to an approach to giving feedback

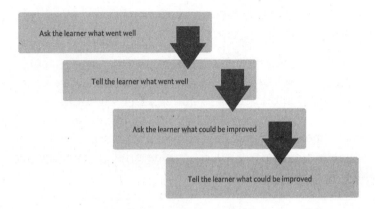

Figure 4. Pendleton's rules of feedback"

where any negative feedback is always sandwiched between two pieces of good feedback. People often describe this as the "sh**t sandwich".

A client told me that there is a shortened version of this, provided by Ken Blanchard – he of the cheery "Feedback is the breakfast of champions" quote. Blanchard's model did not recommend providing the second slice of bread with the second bit of positive feedback. So what you got instead was "an open s**t sandwich".

Human brains can be like Velcro; people get used to the negative being associated with the positive, and brace themselves, as their brain screams "Danger, danger!" Then they are firmly stuck in fight or flight, and are not going to find their way round the learning circle.

Taking this "sandwich" approach unwittingly provides a "get out of jail free" bad feedback card.

Imagine the worried manager, looking at an appraisal request. "I have been told to find something the person needs to do better. Let me see, what did they do wrong? There was that rubbish presentation six months ago, I'll mention that."

As a result, the sandwich feels rather judgement laced. People receiving feedback know that some criticism is coming and this is what they are waiting for. Starting with a question about what the feedback receiver thinks of their own performance brings a negative response, along the lines of, "Well, I don't know, but I'm sure you're going to tell me."

If you regularly have people offering helpful feedback without anything else attached, you will get used to it and be comfortable about it. If it comes in the form of an annual judgemental "sandwich", people will always be waiting for their manager to get to the bit they really want to talk about (i.e. whatever they have done wrong.) Consequently, people will carry on ignoring the good bits wrapped around the sandwich, because those bits aren't really important; they are just there to bookend the meeting.

A word about neurodiversity

Neurodiversity and how we deal with this at work has an impact on how psychologically safe people feel and how they can process feedback.

Everyone will be different in how feedback lands with them and will process it in different ways. There will be an impact due to different backgrounds and experiences, as we have discussed in earlier chapters. In addition to our identity stories, our relationship with the person giving feedback and our ability to "wrong spot" feedback (that is, to find fault with it) will also have an impact.

However, it is also useful to be aware that your own brain

works in a particular way. If there is another person you find it difficult to communicate with and give feedback to, this can be because their brain works very differently to yours.

It may therefore be helpful to consider neurodiversity.

If you are managing a neurodiverse person

There are certain conditions to consider when giving or receiving feedback. This is not the place to discuss different neurodiverse conditions in detail. However, making assumptions (such as "Batu is lazy" because he doesn't seem to sit still, concentrating at his desk for very long) is never helpful. You have no idea why Batu does not sit still for long. Nor can you assume that he is not concentrating. He may need to move around to think, because he has a bad back, varicose veins or an attention deficit hyperactivity disorder (ADHD).

If not sitting still for long has no impact on his work, it really doesn't matter. Make efforts to understand the impact of the corporate culture in your organisation so that you will know when it is pushing you into cultural norms that might impact how you feel about behaviours that seem outside the norm.

If Batu *does* have a particular neurodiverse issue to take into account (for example, an ADHD brain), find out more about what this means for him. Consider what he does well and how you can benefit from more of these.[12] Does he have some particular skills that could be useful to the organisation?

If there are tasks that he finds more difficult, find out what these are and what might help him. If concentration is an issue, explore different techniques to manage this.[13]

Discussing this with the other team members, with his

permission, may also be useful. You might consider speaking to your HR team and asking about wellness action plans designed to encourage employees to share mental health issues and conditions, together with ideas about what would help manage these issues and conditions upfront.[14] The aim is to ensure people stay healthy at work. It will make giving feedback easier, because you'll be able to discuss what would help with the neurodiverse condition as part of your feedback.

For example, "I know you mentioned in your wellness action plan that you wanted me to alert you if I noticed your tasks were not being completed in time, so this is what I am doing now. How can I help?"

Be aware that some neurodiverse conditions mean it is hard for some people to process feedback. Some people may be overly sensitive to feedback; it may feel like the end of the world for them.

No one has the right to insist that people respond to feedback in a particular way. At work, however, you do have the right to comment on the impact of their behaviour and the impact it has on you, the team and/or the work you are doing together.

The key is to learn the right skills, so you can have these discussions in a way that leaves all members of your team feel psychologically safe. As a result they will feel comfortable learning from feedback at work.

Remember

- The culture of an organisation has a significant impact on how useful feedback can be.
- Psychologically safe organisations will enable people to give and receive good feedback.

- Organisations where people are fearful and apportion blame impede learning.
- Leadership has an important role to play in building a culture that enables learning.
- Leaders must model behaviours by seeking and acting on feedback.
- Clarity around expectations is critical if feedback is to be helpful.
- It is important to consider the organisation's approach to neurodiverse conditions and the impact of this on learning.

PART 3

How to give good feedback

By now, you will have explored a lot of information and taken on board some new ideas. (Unless you have just skipped to this point in the book, in which case, welcome.)

Among all this, you should have developed some thoughts about:

- what giving good feedback means
- what helps you do it well
- what might get in the way for you, personally
- what might help or hinder you in your organisation.

Take a moment to note down the key points you have learned so far. How do you now bring all this to life and make it useful for you in your workplace?

You may be feeling perfectly equipped to stride off into the workplace sunset, happily using all this learning to give good feedback. Or you may be wondering where to start.

The important next step is to work out what you need to do now, to try your learning out in the real world and move round the learning circle.

Part 3 helps with this stage by exploring practical models and checklists for you to use on the ground. This section has more of a workbook feel than the previous two and is designed to be something you can turn to and use when planning feedback conversations. The key areas to consider as you put all your learning into practice are:

1. **preparation:** being clear
2. **anticipation:** being helpful

3. **implementation:** being human.

At the end of each of the next three chapters, you will find a checklist to help you consider the different challenges of each of these three stages. You can use these to work through your own individual examples, as well as the examples provided. At the end of the book is a "Have you thought of everything?" checklist for giving good feedback. This will remind you of which chapter to look at as you consider different feedback conversations. You might like to keep a copy of this on your desk or next to your computer for easy reference.

One more thing. If you are still not convinced about how damaging poor feedback can be and how important it is to do it well at work, try Googling "bad feedback". One of the more entertaining threads on Twitter asked people to introduce themselves using the worst piece of feedback they had ever been given. So, as we start to think about how to put all your new skills into action, I have gathered these ideas together in the form of a "found poem".[1] I hope this will help concentrate your mind as you plan your feedback conversations.

Ode to Bad Feedback

A found poem

Hi
My name is Cheryl
I look like I wouldn't be able
To put up with a crushing workload
I'm also too ambitious
And I look a bit too much
Like someone else

I'm Craig
I need to speak up more
When I think something is wrong
But also need to stop being overly assertive
And scary
Hi I'm Amy
I am unpolished
And I have an inherently aggressive Welsh accent
I need to sit on my hands more
If I want to be taken seriously
I'm Alan
I need to stop writing tutorials
Because it is affecting the sales of
Training packages in Australia
And I'll never get promoted with that attitude
Hi I'm Jeremy
I could be doing more
To integrate into the workplace social structure
But I am surprisingly competent
For a Cooperative Extensions Specialist
Actually, no, wait, I'm Dave
I'm a typical Navy reservist
Just not as brilliant
As I think I am
I'm Kevin
I'm an underachiever
I should just calm down
Go back to my office
And meditate
On this feedback

And how useful
It really
Isn't

Read on to make sure that the feedback you offer never appears in one of the Twitter threads like this.

7

Preparation: being clear

You may have noticed a recurring theme of this book: the only helpful feedback is clear feedback. Even commentators who are not entirely on board with using the term "feedback" recommend having regular one-to-one meetings with team members, so that you can offer plenty of clear, real-time reactions to their behaviour.

As you work through this chapter, you will find four key steps to make sure you get off to a flying start to giving crystal-clear, timely feedback. These will build into a checklist, with a full checklist at the end of the chapter.

These four steps are:

1. gather your data
2. interrogate your data
3. write it down
4. plan your process and follow up.

When you put this book down and go back to your office (or sit in front of your computer screen), what does "being clear" mean? What are you actually saying?

In the rush that organisational life often is, it can be easy to slip into vague, confusing pronouncements, disguised as feedback, leaving the other person confused and stuck rather than supported round the learning circle. Even the most skilled and experienced of feedback givers are guilty of this sometimes.

While trying to work out how to be clear, many people delay, tying themselves into so many knots that the (potential but ungiven) feedback gets progressively less and less helpful. How can you get started? The first step to clarity is to gather your feedback data.

Step 1. Gather your data

Let's begin by having a quick refresher of the term "good feedback" and what this means for how you should go about gathering your feedback data.

During this preparation stage, the giving good feedback framework is important, as we are exploring how you can:

- offer your comments on, or reaction to, a particular behaviour that you have observed

- describe the impact of this behaviour on you, the team and/or the work you are trying to produce

- avoid commenting on personality, values, beliefs or attitudes.

As you remind yourself of the giving good feedback framework (Figure 2 in Chapter 1), you may find many obvious examples of behaviour that you want to comment on. However, to turn these into useful feedback data, you will have to make sure that you articulate the behaviour you see and its impact in a way that it is both clear and helpful.

Let's look at some ways to help you do this.

Put your feedback through its PACES

Feedback is always better when it is based on something specific. This makes it so much easier to be clear. The first step is to gather specific examples of observed behaviour.

Then take a step back and review your examples. How can you break them down into clear, helpful learning points?

The answer is by putting your feedback through its PACES.[1]

PACES leads you through a thought process, where you start by challenging your perceptions about what you have observed, then consider in detail what the person is actually doing or not doing, and the consequences of their behaviour on you/the work/work colleagues. You will then be in a much better position to explain your feedback and explore it with the person. Together you can then share ideas and consider what it is about that person's behaviour or actions that either makes them successful or needs to change.

This helps you to follow the good feedback framework, as it forces you to focus in detail on the observed behaviour and its impact, rather than on the other person's personality or unfortunate attitude or the way they seem to clash with your values or beliefs.

Of course, models and frameworks can appear very straightforward in a book. The challenges come when you try to apply them to the real-life complex person you are trying to deal with in your workplace.

To put your feedback through its PACES, think of a person you work with. What feedback data do you have for them that you find tricky to break down into something clear and helpful? Remember, it is always much easier to give clear feedback if you are very specific.

143

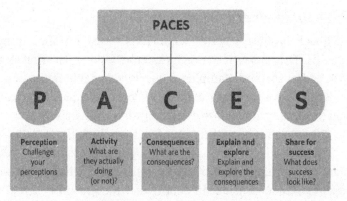

Figure 5. PACES: perception, activity, consequences, explain and explore, share for success

Then move through this question sheet, keeping your example person and their observed behaviour in mind.

QUESTION SHEET 1. THE PACES METHOD

P is for perception: Start by challenging your own perception. What do you think you have observed the person doing? What do you think they are supposed to be doing?

A is for activity: What is happening? What are they actually doing?

C is for consequences: What consequences are there for this behaviour? What is going right and what is going wrong?

E is for explain (and explore): Describe the impact of the behaviour on you/the work/ your colleagues. Use words that show you own the feedback ("I saw", "I noticed", "the impact it had on me was"; not words like "someone mentioned", "the general view is", "most people think")

S is for success (and sharing): What does success look like for both of you/the work? What needs to change to achieve it?

So what was it you asked them to do again? Focus on that. Then you can be clear

---

To make sense of these questions, you probably need to interrogate your data more. That means moving on to Step 2 in the checklist. I'll use an example to help you work through it.

Step 2. Interrogate your data

Maybe you have just had a day at the office where nothing has gone right, and your assistant (let's call him Antoine) hasn't done anything you ask him to do. You know you should give him some feedback. But it feels like every day is like this – there is a litany of things that don't go right and he has an annoying way of ignoring you when you point out mistakes. You are busy and it is tiring even having a normal conversation with him.

As you keep saying to your colleagues (and they all agree with you), there is something wrong with his attitude. He is just very annoying. But you can't give him feedback that he is "just very annoying". You know that will not help him move around the learning circle.

Try as you might, it feels far too hard to articulate the problem. So you deliberately put off any kind of discussion with him. Time goes on. Antoine carries on being very annoying, not getting on with basic tasks but constantly asking you what his key performance indicators are, and wanting feedback on them. By the time someone like me gets involved, you (and your colleagues) are practically gibbering with frustration.

"Help me!" you will say, in a variation of the many conversations held about various shades of Antoine over the years. "He's just really, really annoying. We all think so. He's driving us all demented. And HR say I can't get rid of him until I've started to performance manage him. I've been told to deal with it. I don't know where to start. What am I supposed to say?"

What's going on?

What is your approach in a situation like this? The first step is to get your story straight by gathering your data.

Antoine is fairly new to the workplace and has no idea of the impact of his behaviour on the people around him. If you want to avoid gibbering with frustration when he has no idea about the impact of his attitude, it is up to you to provide that viewpoint for him.

However, you are now in Step 2 of our checklist. Getting your story straight from the start means that you will be spending time in advance, forcing yourself to interrogate your feedback data – that is, the behaviour you have observed and are giving feedback on.

So, what are you trying to say?

I am trying to say that Antoine (insert the name of the person in your team) **is just so annoying** (insert whatever adjective you like)

And now stop, just there. What's happening here?

Starting with this sort of feedback means that you have wandered off down a particular garden path: a path of lazy label and bias, as seen in Chapter 5. You and your colleagues have given Antoine the label "annoying". It is hard for you to interrogate your feedback data when you have that label in your head. Let's try again.

Check your bias

If you are going to give good, clear feedback, you need to move away from the label and the bias. You will have a particular perspective, based on your background and experiences. This will impact the way you interpret behaviour.

Remember, feedback is always about both of you. It often says more about you than the person you are giving the feedback to. Start by questioning yourself.

Ask yourself a few questions beginning with "What"

For example, don't ask "Why is Antoine so annoying?" but "What is Antoine doing to get this reputation?" You can work through quite a few of these questions as you untangle what is going on.

- **What** precisely is it about his attitude that is bothering you?

- **What** is he doing (or not doing) that makes you label him like that?

- **What** are you contributing to this dynamic?

- Is he actually that annoying? Are you really giving him feedback – or are you asking him why he isn't more like you?

Of course, there may be all sorts of reasons why the way Antoine behaves gets under your skin. Only you can work out what they are. If your feedback is to be clear and helpful, you need to give appropriate time and space to this.

Remember that your role, when you are giving feedback, is to help Antoine round the learning circle. If you are to do this, you are focusing on specific behaviours that have an impact on you and the work you and the team are producing.

Write a film script

To help you with the "whats" of the impact rather than the "whys", imagine following Antoine (or your own example person) around, filming the behaviour you are trying to give feedback on and writing a script to go with the film. You are aiming to film scenes that illustrate observed behaviour, relating to Antoine's work.

Using Antoine as an example, the film script might go like this:

You: Antoine, here are the management accounts. Could you please make six copies?

Antoine (taking the accounts from you): Oh, while I have your attention, can I ask when you might have time to sit with me and review my KPIs?

You (turning away): The board meeting is at 3pm. Please go and make the copies.

Antoine: Shall I book a time with your secretary? Or do you use Callendly to make appointments?

You (closing the office door): I need these copies by 2pm at the latest.

Silence. Antoine hovers annoyingly outside your office for about ten minutes.

Once you have written the script, go back and make it more detailed by answering the questions in Question sheet 2.

QUESTION SHEET 2. INTERROGATE YOUR DATA: FILM SCRIPT

- What is the person actually doing or not doing?
- What do you see them doing or not doing?
- What is happening that you can see as a result?
- What is going right and what is going wrong?
- Describe the impact of the behaviour on you and on the work
- Use words that show you own the feedback ("I saw", "I noticed", "the impact it had on me was")

Let's use these questions to put your feedback through its PACES.

What are you trying to say? Stop and think.

P is for perception: Start by challenging your own perception. What do you think you have observed Antoine doing? What do you think he is supposed to be doing?

Antoine is a new trainee with a random number of assigned tasks. The tasks assigned to him, which relate to you, are to support you with admin duties. Your perception is that he isn't doing this, and he is not supporting you in any way

A is for activity: What is he supposed to be doing? What is he actually doing?

You want him just to follow your instructions. This morning you asked him to make six copies of the management accounts. He didn't go to do what you asked, but instead asked for a meeting to discuss his KPIs. You are stressed about the board meeting and have your own work to do; you do not have time to answer lots of questions about basic instructions. You might as well just make the copies yourself

C is for consequences: What consequences are there for this behaviour? What is going right and what is going wrong?

The copies have not been made yet. He is not doing what you have asked, so you are stressed and feel you need to add his duties to your own work. You are feeling pressurised into a different discussion (about his KPIs) which you do not want to have

E is for explain: Explain in detail the consequences and impact of this behaviour

He is asking questions and not getting on with the work you have assigned to him. Now he is hovering outside instead of going away and carrying out your instructions. This has the impact for you of making you feel stressed and extremely unlikely to ask him to do anything else if you can avoid it

S is for success: What does this look like for Antoine/both of you/the work? What needs to change to achieve it?

You just want him to do what he's told. All he has to do is get on with it

Now check back your answers above. Are you being clear?

It is important to remember that in offering feedback, you are not providing Antoine with an objective, universal truth. It may well be that everyone in the company thinks he is annoying. But what you are preparing now is feedback data. This covers the impact of what you have gathered on your "film", the examples of specific behaviours on that particular day, and the impact of them on you and on the work you are aiming to provide together. This is offered to Antoine to help him learn.

So, does this feedback feel fair to you? Have you really put it through its PACES? Are you sure? Do you need to do a bit more to explore as well as explain? And to share instead of just offering your view of success? What was it you asked him to do again?

And what happened then? This is the thing to focus on

Now you have a method available to help gather and interrogate your feedback data.

But, as part of your preparation stage, and getting your story straight, there are a few more things to consider if your clear feedback is to be as helpful as possible. Writing down your feedback will help you clear your mind and see things from a broader perspective.

Having completed that, we will now move to Step 3 of the checklist.

Step 3. Write it down

Beware recency bias

This leads us to consider another common sin that many people commit when giving feedback. This is falling victim to the "recency" effect. In other words, the times when you offer hastily concocted generalised comments, based entirely on one event last week. Sometimes you might add insult to injury by suggesting that this is an indication of how this person "always" behaves, claiming they are "always" doing X or "never" doing Y. Comments like this are never helpful.

The point at which this effect generally seems to occur is when people are asked to provide written feedback by others, for example as part of a formal process such as ratings or appraisals. Then strange things happen to their carefully sourced and interrogated feedback data and all their best practice learning goes right out of the window.

Perhaps this is because many people find these processes difficult and time consuming, so they allow the pressure of the formal process to negate all the previous advice, leave any preparation until the last minute and then try and cobble together something that fits whatever kind of system they are dealing with.

Avoid being pushed into this approach. Get ahead of the game and be able to whip out clear, well-considered feedback data whenever someone asks for a rating or appraisal by writing down your feedback as you go along.

Look for trends and patterns

Trends and patterns (the ones that tend to lead to unhelpful labels if you don't put the work in to analyse them) will be easier to illustrate clearly if you have a data bank of feedback and can offer other examples of times when this behaviour has been demonstrated. This makes it much clearer and is a much better way of helping people round the learning circle.

So, going back to Antoine, don't just close the office door in his face or say, "You are always asking for KPIs instead of getting on with the work. Just go away, will you?"

Instead, provide clear feedback along the following lines. "I have noticed a pattern over the last month where every day I have asked you to complete X and this has not been completed. You have still asked about your KPIs and I have explained that your KPIs are actually the completion of X. The impact of this is ..."

Keeping a written record of regular feedback will mean you always have your story straight. It can also help you see inconsistencies in your data, and make it easy to spot and discuss behaviour patterns at work. To do this, you need to get into good habits.

We are now going to move on to Step 4 of the checklist.

Step 4. Plan your process and follow up

Now you have gathered all your clear feedback and got your feedback story straight, what you are going to do with the data? What process will you put in place to make sure it remains helpful to the person and supports them round the learning circle?

Ask yourself the following questions.

- What records of the feedback are you required to keep?
- What follow up do you need to put in place? How will you check development/ progress/ further examples of the behaviour you have identified and the impact of it?
- Does this link with any organisational process?
- What impact do the organisational processes have on the feedback? Do they help or hinder?
- What might you have to do to build on where they help and to mitigate when they hinder?

Let's look at another example to illustrate the power of writing down your feedback and putting a follow-up process in place.

You work with Mateo who is, in many ways, very capable. His role is to find some outreach opportunities for the organisation and provide support with them. He is driving you all to distraction by the way he seems to think he can boss you all around and tell you all what to do. You don't want to be too negative (you know he tries.) But you are worried about his reaction to any feedback. He frightens you a bit, not to put too fine a point on it. He seems so judgemental and bossy, and you know you shouldn't be labelling him like that, so you have put off telling him what you think.

You also know that it's important he understands the pressure he is putting on others and that he needs to improve his relationship with the team. You are finding it extremely difficult to know what feedback you should write down.

Written feedback

Your organisation requires you to offer written feedback every few months. The fourteenth nagging request has come in from HR and you cannot avoid it any longer. You pore over your comments for hours. You are quite pleased with the written feedback you have come up with.

> Mateo has an ambitious attitude towards the organisation. He has lots of ideas, in particular about the achievements and results we can achieve. This includes a drive for continuous improvement for us all. This approach is full of ambition and determination and Mateo is good at what he does. However, he is frequently negative and puts much pressure on both himself and the team to overachieve. This includes high expectations for things that sometimes are just not possible. This adds increased pressure and creates anxiety. If he does less, for example just do what he has been asked, then he and the team would be less stressed. This will enable him to be more positive, focus on the good things we do and enjoy the work more. Also, he makes multiple requests for the same information across the team and this can be frustrating.

Be clear: what are you trying to say here? Let's write it down again, putting it through its PACES.

Perception

Your perception is that Mateo has been asked – to do what exactly?

Is there confusion about the scope of a particular task or project you are giving feedback on, confusion about his role generally, or confusion about both? Can you tell from the feedback above?

It is hard to give clear feedback if there is no clarity about what someone is supposed to be doing.

Written feedback gives you the opportunity to take a step back and interrogate the data from a more holistic perspective. Perhaps, before you give the feedback, you need to make sure that you have made his responsibilities clear.

For example, "Mateo's specific role with the organisation is to find x number of outreach opportunities and provide support (in the form of ....) for them."

Activity

What is it that you think he is supposed to be doing?

For example, "to agree the opportunities, set them up and make sure they run smoothly by doing xyz".

What is he actually doing?

For example, "We have a budget for three events. Mateo discovered 30 local opportunities, agreed our involvement with the organisers and then asked various team members to join in and provide support. He has been very organised and enthusiastic. However, we had a budget for three events, not 30. Mateo tried to get team members involved in new events that he had unilaterally decided were important, but which were not in budget."

Consequences

What is going right and what is going wrong? Explain the impact of what he is doing or not doing.

For example, "There have been three events which have achieved their goal. There have been 27 events Mateo wanted team members to attend which were not a priority for us, as they were not in budget. Mateo did not take on board the instruction and continued to pressurise team members to attend events not in their time budget. This impacted on the team, adding stress due to multiple requests for time spent out of the office. Mateo followed these requests by attending the events on his own and publicly criticising staff members for not joining in, for example yesterday saying that staff are not committed to the organisation because they did not agree to join the event. He can't believe how lazy they are. This has had the impact of making the members of staff criticised feel bullied and not listened to."

Explore for Success

You can use this feedback as an opportunity to start again. Leaving aside the clarity or otherwise of his role, it sounds as though Mateo is unaware of his impact, so some short, written feedback, followed by exploratory discussions about the impact of his behaviour, will help him reflect on and revisit the feedback data you have prepared for him. It also gives you the ability to share your ideas for success and talk about patterns of behaviour, and follow up if his approach to event planning does not settle down after a time.

Plan your process and follow up

By writing down this detail, that feedback now seems clearer. What do you need to put in place as your follow-up process?

Booking regular catch-ups for Mateo would have helped in this instance and will help in the future. By having these in place, you will be able to share regular feedback on the impact of his approach, and steer or correct as you go along. This will make your feedback more helpful and will support him round the learning circle.

As this follow-up was not in place before, he is getting the feedback a while after the event and you have ended up providing the strange feedback sandwich, which takes away as much as it gives.

Being clear: final points

Practice makes perfect. As you embark on the preparation stage of your feedback journey, you can make sure you don't miss a trick by working through Checklist 1 to prepare your crystal-clear feedback.

Antoine (or whoever is your own example) may still be annoying; Mateo may still frighten you a bit. But you now have a practical take-away in the form of a structure you can use to interrogate your data and break down the behaviour into helpful, clear, constructive examples. As a result, you will understand more of what is going on for both of you, and you will both have the best chance to learn and grow.

CHECKLIST 1. PREPARATION: BEING CLEAR

Step 1. Gather your data: what am I trying to say?
Use the giving good feedback framework
How can I describe this in terms of the person's behaviour?
What examples have I observed of this behaviour?

Put your feedback through its PACES
- **P is for challenging your perceptions:** What do you think is happening? What do you think should be happening?
- **A is for activity:** What are they actually doing?
- **C is for consequences:** What is happening as a result? What is going right and wrong?
- **E is for explaining (and exploring)** in detail the impact on you/the team/the work
- **S is for success (and sharing):** What does this look like for both of you/the work? What needs to change to achieve success?

Step 2. Interrogate your data
Imagine you are following this person around and filming them. What would you notice when you watch the film? What would you write down as a film script?
What is the person actually doing? What do you see them doing or not doing?
What is happening that you can see as a result of what they are doing or not doing?
What is going right and what is going wrong?
Describe the impact, on you, the work, or the team of the behaviour
Describe the impact in words that you can own

Check your bias
Review your film script. Consider what you have contributed to this dynamic
- What is it that you have noticed that is bothering you?
- What is the person doing that makes you label them in any way?
- What are you contributing to this dynamic?
- Are you really giving feedback? Or are you asking why they aren't more like you?

Step 3. Write it down
- Write down your feedback
- Review your feedback data from a broader perspective (patterns/themes)
- Do this regularly to avoid recency bias

Step 4. Plan your process and follow up
Manage your data to support the person moving round the learning circle
- Where and how are you going to keep it? How will you follow up?
- Put a regular follow-up process in place

8

Anticipation: being helpful

Now you have explored your feedback data in some detail, you have practised articulating it clearly and you have your story straight. As far as the "what" of giving good feedback goes, it is job done. You can set off to give your crystal-clear feedback, feeling perfectly confident about what you have to say.

Or can you?

Is there anything else you need to consider, to make sure that this feedback is super helpful?

What about the conversation you need to have? Have you thought much about that?

Anticipating any feedback conversation is important. Getting your story straight is a great starting point, but it is just the start. Feedback is never something you just hand over as you run for the hills. The real foundations for learning are in the **feedback discussion**.

The discussion is the point at which you can support people best in moving round the learning circle. It is also the point at which you can fall flat on your face, with all your carefully prepared feedback data crashing to the floor next to you.

Helpful feedback conversations should stay in a forward-thinking, constructive space. This can be difficult if you are blindsided by the whole new layer of dynamics that come with the discussion.

So, before heading off to give good feedback, spend time considering how to approach your feedback discussions and be well prepared for whatever might come up. By doing this, you will address the next points in our definition of feedback, i.e. how you can:

- explore your feedback via a helpful discussion, and therefore
- support movement around the learning circle.

As you work through this chapter, you will explore four key steps to make sure you get off to a flying start to holding helpful feedback discussions. We will build these into a checklist as we go along and you will be able to see the full checklist at the end of the chapter.

The four steps to consider are:

1. how you will communicate the data – your communication approach
2. how the other person might react
3. how this might affect you
4. how you will move the conversation forward.

In other words, at this stage, you are moving from thinking about what your feedback is to focusing on how you are going to communicate it. You can see the way this can work in Figure 6 on the next page.

As before, ideas and models can seem straightforward when you look at them on the page. How can you put them into practice with your real-life people? Let's look at some practical steps to help you move through the four steps and answer the questions above.

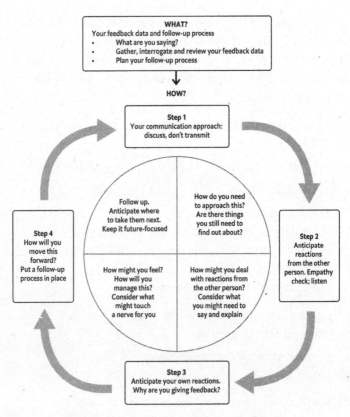

Figure 6. Moving from "what" to "how": planning a helpful feedback conversation

Step 1. Your communication approach

How do you need to approach this conversation? How are you going to communicate the data you have so carefully gathered? Are there things you still need to find out about?

Move from transmission to discussion

To answer these questions, you need to be well equipped to make a shift from transmission mode to discussion mode.

Transmission is an understandable state to get into when you are giving feedback. It's an unfortunate side effect of many an appraisal or rating process. If you have spent a lot of time carefully researching and interrogating your feedback data, you naturally want the person to listen and understand what you have to say.

The purpose of the conversation is not, however, to impress people with your data-gathering skills or have them fall at your feet in grateful appreciation of the time you have spent considering their feedback. You are offering them your reaction to, or comment on, a particular behaviour or action and its impact on you or the work you are doing together. You are doing this in the spirit of helpfulness, to help them learn. It is important not to be so pleased with yourself that you forget to focus on responding to *their* reactions, rather than giving *your* feedback.

Improve the pace: explore as well as explain

To help with this transformation, you need to keep improving the way you put your feedback through its PACES. So, as you start discussing your feedback, you need to spend as much time exploring it with the person as explaining. Work through your examples to anticipate what the person might have to say about your feedback and how you might go about managing this conversation helpfully. This will also help to shift your thinking in advance from transmission mode to discussion mode. As a result, your feedback (and your mindset going into the discussion) will be more forward looking and constructive.

When you are anticipating your discussion around your observed behaviours, consider these exploratory questions.

- What is their take on this?
- What could they do differently?
- What are the different options?
- What could success look like?
- What difference would this make?

As soon as you get into the conversation and ask: "What is your take on this?", you are in uncharted territory. If you are about to head into a conversation, it is worth role playing in your head the different scenarios you might have to deal with.

Are there still things you need to find out about?

Let's work this idea through with Antoine, from our earlier example. He has been annoying you, hovering outside your office all morning, asking about his KPIs instead of doing what you have asked. You have kept a log of all the other times he has demonstrated this annoying behaviour, and because he has just done it again, you decide you will have a conversation with him about it. You ask him to come in and sit down.

You offer Antoine the following (carefully thought through and practised) feedback.

> "I have noticed a pattern over the last month where every day I have asked you to complete a task (e.g. photocopying documents, like today) and you have not done so. Instead, you have asked about your KPIs and asked to book a meeting to discuss your KPIs. Your KPIs are actually the completion

of the basic tasks I set (e.g. the completed photocopies). When you do not complete them, that creates problems. If documents are not copied, or are only given to me at the last minute before my meetings, I have no time to check them. The impact of this is that I feel concerned that we may not get our full budget next year, as I do not have the correct copies (and therefore the correct data) available to discuss with the board."

You make sure that you are not just in transmission mode, and ask for his input.

"What's your take on this? What could you do differently?"

What do you think Antoine's reaction is likely to be?

- He might say, "Oh I'm so sorry, I read this management book which said communicating in KPIs was a good way to talk to your boss. I'll just get on with what you ask me to do in future."

- He might burst into tears and say, "I'm so anxious, this is my first job, no one has really told me what to do. Are you telling me I'm fired?"

- He might become defensive or angry and say, "What do you mean? You have been ignoring me for months. I think you hate me. I'm going to HR."

You will have to respond appropriately to whatever he comes back with. You don't know, of course, what this will be. In fact, you don't know Antoine very well, so it could be anything. You could be left staring like a surprised goldfish as you offer him tissues and wonder what to say next.

How can you anticipate the unknown so that you can be as

helpful as possible? For a start, you do have to be interested in Antoine and what is going on for him. Why do you think he keeps asking about his KPIs?

It is time to move on to Step 2 of our checklist – considering the reactions from the other person.

Step 2. Reactions from the other person

How might you deal with reactions from the other person? Consider things you might need to be prepared to say or explain.

As you continue to put your feedback through its PACES, remember that Success also means Sharing.

What's their perspective?

We are often so busy being outraged, irritated or offended by someone else's behaviour, or worried or embarrassed by a missed deadline or incident, that we give feedback based purely on how *we* are feeling, from *our own* perspective.

You cannot anticipate your conversation unless you have considered the feelings and perspective of the person you are giving feedback to. If you have no idea how the person is likely to react, you have probably not taken enough interest in them.

It's entirely possible that the person you're talking to has a completely different view of the situation you are giving feedback about. They haven't had the feedback yet, so they don't know your reaction to their presentation or don't understand your embarrassment at their lack of awareness with the client at that meeting.

As part of anticipating your helpful conversation, you need to develop some empathy. You can do this by doing an empathy check, in the following way.[1]

Go back to the very specific behaviour you have observed and consider these questions.

- What sort of relationship do you have with the person?
- What did you observe yourself doing and saying during the observed behaviours you "filmed" earlier?
- What did they do and say?
- What do you notice about how you were thinking and feeling?
- How might they have been thinking and feeling?
- How do you think your feedback is likely to land with them?

Try this with the example person you thought about in the last chapter. You may find that asking yourself these questions changes your view about the feedback and your relationship with them.

Are you listening?

To give good feedback, it is important to continue to develop your relationship with the people you're giving that feedback to.

In any good relationship, you have to communicate well. Are you on the same page as the person you are talking to? How do you know?

The best way to communicate (and so the best way to anticipate good feedback conversations) is to listen.

Really listen.

There is a distinct difference between *listening* and *hearing*.

Hearing is easy, accidental and involuntary. People can do it without thinking about it, just as many of us can drive without thinking about it. For example, you can get all the way home on a familiar journey in auto-pilot mode, with no memory of passing particular landmarks. Even if you wanted to, you cannot avoid overhearing the occasional conversation going on at the next table in a restaurant or behind you on public transport. But you generally don't take notes or turn round to look at them.

Listening is focused, voluntary and intentional. When you listen, you use all your senses, you look at what the person is telling you in the words they use and in their body language, expressions, actions. You remember what they say, ask questions, reflect back the main points and agree what they want to happen at the end of a conversation.

Stay focused

Feedback can be complicated. You can start off talking about one thing and then something else gets into the mix. When this happens, as it often will, you can end up going off down an unhelpful garden path. The result can be an argument about something one of you considers important but the other person thinks irrelevant to the conversation.

For example, you want talk to Fung about her confusing approach to preparing management accounts, which has meant that you and the team do not have the financial information you need to hand. Fung wants to talk about how hard she has been working and how impossible it is to get the information for the accounts in the first place. She talks about working all night for weeks, bursts into tears, the conversation gets complicated and clear communication stops.

It may often be the case that, as part of the discussion, new issues are raised that need dealing with. However, if you are listening actively, you will note the new issues and acknowledge them. To keep the conversation on track, you need to make clear that you are dealing first with one issue and then the other.

Listening is an active, involved process. When you are listening, you do not take anything for granted. You listen to what is said and ask questions until you understand.

When was the last time you communicated like this with a team member? When have you been so wrapped up your own internal dialogue that you have not listened to what the person is saying? Check the next time you feel slightly distracted. Can you repeat back to them what they have just said? Do you understand what they mean? Are you sure?

Plan to work hard at listening, so that you can be helpful. Use the steps shown in Figure 7 to help anticipate the conversation and share the different paths to success.

1. **Frame the conversation**
   "I want to talk about ...; I want you to know ..."

2. **Acknowledge their comments**
   "I think I heard you say ..."

3. **Check you have got it right**
   "Have I heard you properly? Is that the right summary of the issues you have raised?"

4. **Make sure they have heard your feedback about what you value, the impact of their behaviour on you and the work you do together**
   "First of all, let me say, I value your (details of work) and I think it is always going to be useful to the organisation."

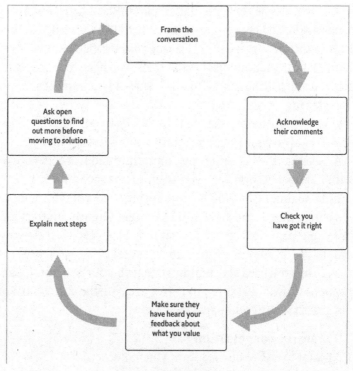

Figure 7. Active listening

5. **Explain next steps**

"So I'd like to take the time to explore both points in some detail before we move to looking at any solutions. Let's start with ..."

6. **Ask open questions to find out more before moving to the solution**

"Can you tell me more about that? How can we help? What would be best for you?"

Knowing more, you will be better able to agree solutions.

Have a think about the person you identified in Chapter 7. How well do you listen to them? Could you imagine working through the steps above with them? What might they say? How might they react?

Listening: an example

Let's look at an example to help practise this approach.

You are discussing a client meeting you attended with a valued team member, Ivona. In the meeting, Ivona was distracted and missed several opportunities to follow up with the client about new sales. This is not like her; usually she is very on the ball. You managed to jump in, so opportunities were not lost, but you are worried about this happening at other meetings when you are not there. You offer her feedback about the behaviour you noticed and ask for her reaction.

Ivona takes a deep breath. Then she launches into a long monologue about feeling stressed. You hear her say something about moving on; it will be best for the organisation, she says.

Your heart sinks. This is the third time you have had to recruit for this role. What a shame, she is such a good employee. But there we are. You aren't really surprised she wants to move on; no one stays in this role for long. You have been expecting this for some time.

"OK, Ivona," you say. "Don't worry. I'll be sorry to lose you; I understand."

Stop here. You are not listening.

You will of course be sorry to lose her, she is a great asset. But you do not really understand her yet, do you? You haven't asked any questions. She said she was feeling stressed. Did you listen? What do you know about that? What is going on for her? What is making her stressed now? What is different at this point, compared with this time last year, when everything was fine? What can you do to help?

You have heard the conversation. But you have not really listened. You are too wrapped up in your own internal dialogue (this is a difficult role, no one stays for long, here we go again, more recruitment).

There are two separate issues here. Obviously, you will take whatever action is needed to make sure the organisation continues to function. That is your job as a manager.

But looking after a valued staff member is your job too. You have offered feedback, she has offered her resignation in return. That was probably not your intended outcome. Did you remember to move away from your viewpoint when you were giving her that feedback? Or were you so focused on the potential loss of sales that you forgot that this behaviour was very much a one-off?

First, you need to know what's going on for her. You have to show Ivona that you care. She thinks you are criticising her and saying she isn't good enough. Resigning is her solution.

You need to find out more. Then you can discuss potential solutions, both for her and the organisation. When you stop to think about it, you know it is best for the organisation if she stays in her role.

To find out more, you have to listen differently.

1. **Frame the conversation**
   "I want to talk about your decision to resign. I want you to know that your work is usually great. For example ..."
   Your first task is to let Ivona know where you are coming

from. You know she tends to shrug off compliments and looks slightly stressed if you make her listen to them. So tell her that her work is generally fine and why it is fine.

2. **Acknowledge her comments**
"I think I heard you say two things ..."

She seems to be telling you two things in response to your feedback that she did not seem quite herself at the meeting.

1. She is stressed.
2. She thinks it is best for the organisation if she moves on.

Telling you these things may be her indirect way of asking for help and support. It is up to you to help her learn a way of communicating more directly by building that relationship through asking questions.

3. **Check you have got it right**
"Have I heard you properly? Is that the right summary of the issues you have raised?"

4. **Make sure she has heard your feedback about what you value, the impact of her behaviour on you and the work you do together**
"First of all, let me say, I value your work and commitment (give specific details of what you value and examples of when you have seen it) and I think it is always going to be useful to the organisation. I really do not want to lose you."

5. **Explain next steps**
"So I'd like to take the time to explore both points in some detail before we move to looking at any solutions. Let's start with ..."

6. **Ask open questions to find out more before moving to the solution**

"Can you tell me more about that? How can we help? What would be best for you?"

Once you have found out more, you will be in a better position to agree solutions.

When you're sure you are able to listen properly and understand the other person's perspective, you can move on to Step 3 of the checklist – your potential reactions to the feedback discussion.

Step 3. Reactions from you

How do you feel about the conversation? How will you manage the issues you can see might come up? Consider things that may touch a nerve for you.

While you are describing the impact of some behaviour on you, you also have to consider your contribution to the situation and the resulting dynamic. Often your reaction to the behaviour you have observed can get in the way of being helpful. You can get then get firmly stuck in transmission mode.

Why are you giving feedback?

To guard against this, ask yourself why you are having this particular conversation and giving this particular feedback right now. The answer is important in anticipating your contribution to the dynamic and thus your likely reactions during the conversation.

There can be a whole host of reasons why you might want to give feedback at work.

- You might be angry about some bad behaviour, or embarrassed when you feel a junior colleague has let you down in a meeting.

- You might want to praise someone who you think is very important to your team.

- It might be rating time and HR have told you to gather feedback for your team, and you guiltily realise there are all sorts of points you should have raised before.

- You could be the victim of "feedback buck passing" which can be rife in some companies; for example, your boss saying, "Sort Kareem out will you? He's a nightmare," or, "Tatyana's always off, isn't she? Lazy and slow. We can't carry people like that. Get on to it, will you?"

Just stop for a moment, and consider your reasons. It is very easy, under pressure from your emotions, colleagues or organisational processes to be bounced into bad habits. Then you can end up in unhelpful conversations, offering generalised, unhelpful feedback, perhaps based on personality, which has no chance of helping the person around the learning circle.

Let's go back to Chapter 1 and remind ourselves what feedback is all about.

Feedback is always about communication. In a simple communication loop, it shows you have been heard and understood.

We also know that feedback is all about learning, and so you want the feedback you communicate to be helpful and support people around the learning circle.

It is important to "say it" but that does not mean you should rush to give feedback without proper preparation and careful anticipation. Not all feedback is equally useful. Make your feedback count.

There will be some key questions to ask yourself first, listed in Question sheet 3.

QUESTION SHEET 3. WHY AM I GIVING FEEDBACK?

What has triggered your decision to give this feedback now?
- Detail the behaviour, incident, action, emotion, organisational process

What outcome are you hoping for?
- For example, a shared understanding of how to behave in a particular situation, different behaviour in the next meeting, a project plan so that things are better organised next time

What sort of feedback is this?
- For example, appreciation of some good work, a follow-up to instructions that have not been followed closely enough, coaching to develop skills for the future, evaluation for an organisational process

---

Focusing on outcomes is an important way of checking in on yourself, your motivation and your emotional state. (To be clear, a desire to pass on the blame so that you feel better is not an acceptable outcome to wish for, and does not indicate a helpful emotional state.)

At this point, you should remain future focused and helpful. To do this, it is important to diffuse some of your emotions about the situation.

If someone else has asked you to give feedback to a member of your team, feel free to push it back politely. You can suggest they work through the feedback using the checklists provided, and then give the feedback themselves.

You can also use a technique such as Douglas Stone and Sheila Heen's "system lens" to review the situation from a more dispassionate perspective.[2] This helps you to take different steps away from the immediate action.

One step back. In what ways does the feedback reflect differences in preferences, assumptions, styles or implicit rules between us?

Two steps back. Do our roles make it more or less likely that we might bump into each other?

Three steps back. What other players influence our behaviour and choices? Are physical set-ups, processes or structures also contributing to the problem?

Circling back to me. What am I doing or failing to do that is contributing to the dynamic between us?

Try this with the example person you have identified. Does this model offer any insights into what *you* might be contributing to the situation?

With Antoine, you could use this model to take the annoyance (i.e. your emotional labelling of his behaviour) out of the equation and work out what you have contributed to this.

One step back. Antoine asks about his KPIs because he is making the assumption that there is a plan he is not part of. He is not used to the world of work and he has not yet understood many implicit rules of the organisation.

Two steps back. Your roles (Antoine, as peripatetic trainee, and you, as manager of many trainees) mean that you are in conflict. He expects a lot of support and learning; you expect to do the minimum, as there will be another trainee next week.

Three steps back. He is used to the idea of things being competitive and needing to prove himself via grades and numbers. He got onto the graduate programme via exams. He is waiting for marks out of ten for his weekly tasks. The organisation has no such processes or structures in place. You are not expecting to provide any such thing.

Circling back to you. You have not taken any interest in Antoine. If you take the time to ask him why he keeps asking about his KPIs, you may glean some of the information above and be able to help him.

What kind of feedback is this?

As you consider your feedback conversation, another way to take a step back is to consider what label you would put on the feedback. What kind of feedback are you trying to give?

Appreciation

This type of feedback makes it clear how much you appreciate what someone has done. It's an opportunity to make sure that you are not just offering a bland "Well done" because you want to make sure they have really heard you. You achieve this by taking the time to write down and talk through the person's behaviour or action and its impact on you. It is important that you do this in just as much detail as when your feedback is about course correction.

This lends itself well to moving into a coaching conversation where you invite the other person to consider what they might want to do with this information, what this means for their future career and how they can share their skills with colleagues.

Evaluation

As part of your organisational process, you may be doing an annual or biannual performance evaluation. In this, you are supporting the person by pulling together feedback that they might have received over the year. You are helping them look at patterns, plans, think about what they might like to do in the future, paying attention to their service, bearing witness to their triumphs and disappointments.

Importantly, these performance evaluations should never be the first time that people hear feedback. Nor should they provide the opportunity to pass on aggregated secondhand feedback (e.g. "I've asked around and we all think, Sally, that you are very aggressive.")

This isn't going to help Sally with learning or development. It is not focused enough and doesn't offer her any opportunity to ask questions about examples or times when this behaviour was witnessed. Consequently, there can be no discussion about how she might develop new behaviours. As a result, she won't behave any differently next year.

Steps and instruction

Between these two types of feedback is the feedback you may find yourself offering most frequently, akin to Buckingham and Goodall's steps and instructions: this is how to do something; not like that, like this; don't do this again; this is how we do things around here.

Often this feedback follows on from a set of instructions that need to be reinforced or explained differently. This feedback is not necessarily big each time, but it can build into patterns. So it needs to be clear, specific and given near the time of the behaviour you have observed.

Regular catch-ups with your line reports, using your feedback data, offer perfect opportunities for this sort of feedback. Also, giving feedback regularly prevents it from becoming a mountain that you never climb.

As you anticipate your feedback conversation, consider what sort of feedback the person might be expecting. Is there likely to be some confusion? Have you worked through the different ways in which your feedback could be interpreted?

As an example, someone might say, "I want some feedback, because I just want to know where I stand."

By asking where they stand, they mean they want to be noticed. They are actually asking, "Do you see the efforts I make every day? Do you think I make a difference? Do you notice me? I don't know what impact I have."

But you hear them saying they want to know where they stand, so you swing into a general evaluation of their performance. This leaves them feeling unappreciated.

As a result, it is important to plan how you can add a sprinkling of appreciation into any of the feedback you give. One overriding motivation for going into work might be to pay your gas bill. But most people want to do a good job too, so probably feel they put rather more effort into it than is strictly necessary. Your feedback can help them make sure their efforts are properly targeted.

Question sheets 4, 5 and 6 can help you plan out the different types of conversations.

QUESTION SHEET 4. APPRECIATION

What have they done well? (e.g. the results obtained, the way they approach the work and the relationships they have built with the people involved)

What difference did it make having them do the work rather than someone else?

What unique spikiness do they bring to their work?

You can then move this into a coaching discussion by reflecting back
- What are their thoughts about this?
- How do they see their current role and longer-term career being developed?
- How can they build on their unique spikiness?
- How can they share their skill with colleagues?

QUESTION SHEET 5. EVALUATION

- Evaluate from the point of view of this particular organisation or project
- What factors have helped or hindered the person's performance?
- How can they become more effective now and in the future?
- What practical support and learning or training/development do they need?
- What could they develop in the future?
- What do you think they should avoid doing in the future?
- What plans do they have for their career and development?
- How can you help and support them with these?

QUESTION SHEET 6. STEPS AND INSTRUCTIONS

Put your feedback about observed behaviours through its PACES again
- What is going right and what is going wrong?
- What aspects of your communication/instructions do you need to review?
- What should you avoid doing when you give instructions in the future?
- Are you keeping your "film" of observed behaviours up to date?

What regular meetings can you put in place to discuss these?

What patterns can you see emerging?
How can you talk through these with the person, so that they are helpful?
What thoughts might they have about these?

How will you move all these forward?

Once you have followed Steps 1–3 on our checklist, there is one final step.

This is to make sure that you have paid attention to your process and have put something in place to make sure that you can follow up on your feedback.

So we are now moving on to Step 4 – how to move all these things forward.

Step 4. Moving the conversation forward

To move the conversation forward, you need to keep it future focused. It will often take time for people to take feedback on board and move round the learning circle. One conversation is unlikely to be enough, so it's important that you have in place the kind of follow-up process outlined in Chapter 7. It may take the form of a planned further conversation, a process that means you naturally have regular conversations, or something that's written down.

Plan it in advance and make sure that the feedback and learning does not get lost.

Here's an example to illustrate how you can pull all these things together.

Erika is a perfectly super team member. She is generally great, a superstar in fact, everyone agrees. You know you should tell her this. You want to make sure she feels appreciated. You haven't got round to it yet. You know that just regularly saying "Well done" is not quite enough, but you haven't worked out what else to say.

A meeting with a client goes particularly well. You wonder if you can say something about this? But you do not want to patronise her. It would seem odd to say, "Great relationship building, Erika," when building relationships with clients is a big part of her job. So you don't say anything and, as you dither, the moment passes. Erika carries on doing great work. You are happy and assume she is too. Anyway, she is good at her job, so you reason that maybe you don't really need to worry too much.

Then a new project comes in. You think this will make great use of Erika's skills. It needs someone really organised to keep the team on track, and this is never easy to do. Erika is definitely the best person for the job. You book a meeting with her and take the opportunity to say, "I noticed how well you dealt with client Y. This is a great new project that will make use of your skills."

You are proud of yourself, having managed to remember the previous project, notice her skills and reward her with new work. You feel you have ticked all the feedback boxes.

You are taken aback when Erika seems a bit huffy, and says,

"You've never mentioned my great organisation skills before. In fact, you never give me any feedback. You're only talking to me now because this is a rubbish project, that none of the men want to do, so you think a woman will sort it, don't you?"

What's going on?

Erika is asking to be seen and appreciated. She is also looking to develop her career and thinks she has earned an interesting next project. She has interpreted your efforts at giving appreciative feedback as a smokescreen to dump work on her.

It is important that you hold follow-up conversations with her and take the time to demonstrate to her regularly that you notice exactly what it is that she does well. You can use the appreciative feedback questions to help you prepare these conversations as you notice examples of positive behaviour you want to mention. You also need to make sure you have a process in place to have these conversations regularly.

What have they done well?

This includes the results obtained, the way they approach the work and the relationships they have built with the people involved.

What is it that you have observed her doing that makes her customer service so brilliant? You could say something like,

> "You have been doing some great client work. I noticed the way you put the client at ease yesterday, by taking such care in presenting the information in a way he could hear and understand it. This is a great skill, and unusual on the team. I love it."

What difference did it make having them do the work rather than someone else?

Maybe you have noticed the way she always checks in with clients on a personal level when she sees them, remembers details they have told her about their families.

You could say something like,

> "I noticed the way you offered the Spritzer boss corporate entertainment that matches with the things his family likes as well as his values, offering him and his teenage daughter VIP tickets to the Olly Murs concert, as well as the opportunity

to do some fundraising for their favourite charity. That was genius."

What unique spikiness do they bring to their work?

What do they do that is unique to them and which you really appreciate?

Maybe Erika is very aware of the importance of inclusive behaviour, warm and assertive, so people respect her but don't take advantage.

You could say something like,

> "I wanted to say that you were right to call me out about not giving you feedback often enough and checking that projects with a heavy admin load are not given just to women. I will check myself on that in future and would like you to continue to give me feedback on what you notice. I like the way you have the courage of your convictions and don't shy away from giving difficult feedback."

How can they build on their unique spikiness?

At one of your regular follow-up meetings, you can build on your appreciative feedback to help her consider her future. You can start moving into a coaching discussion.

You could say something like,

> "The way you tune into clients and their needs is a great skill, as we've discussed. What thoughts do you have about how you would like to develop this experience?"

How can they share their skill with colleagues?

You can also help her think about sharing her skills, in a positive way. For example,

> "Erika, the way you encourage us all to focus on inclusive behaviour is fantastic. How would you like to develop this, so that the team continue to learn from your ideas?"

Reflect back. What thoughts do they have about this?

How do they see their current role and longer-term career being developed?

With someone like Erika, someone you appreciate and want to encourage, it is important that you keep up the reflecting back/coaching type of feedback discussions.

For example, "Erika, I've noticed the way you build great relationships with clients. We've talked about four fantastic examples this week. What ideas do you have about how you would like to build on this, for example in relation to projects?"

Or, "What skills would you be interested in developing next year? What projects might help you do this?"

This approach recognises Erika's contribution and avoids her feeling that her only reward for good work is having more work dumped on her. It also helps you find out her feelings on building her career and provides you both with sense of ongoing progress. This keeps the feedback conversation future focused. It is just as important to do this with people who you think are performing well as with those who you think are not.

You have now spent plenty of time anticipating your feedback conversation to make sure that it is as helpful as it possibly can be. Checklist 2 provides a practical takeaway to make sure you have not missed any steps before you go ahead.

CHECKLIST 2. ANTICIPATION: BEING HELPFUL

Step 1. Your communication approach
Move from transmission to discussion

Get into the right mindset by checking your PACES. Consider these questions:

E for explore and explain

- What is their take on this?
- What could they do differently?
- What are the different options?

S for share for success

- How do they think they can adapt/build on/develop their behaviours or actions?
- What difference would this make?
- What would success look like, for both of you?
- Are there still things you need to find out about?

Step 2. Reactions from the other person
What's their perspective?
Empathy check

- What did you do and say during the observed behaviours you "filmed" earlier?
- What did they do and say?
- What do you notice about how you were thinking and feeling?
- How might they have been thinking and feeling?
- How might this impact what you saw?

Are you listening?

- Frame the conversation
- Acknowledge their comments
- Check you have got it right
- Make sure they have heard your feedback about what you value, the impact of their behaviour on you and the work you do together
- Explain next steps
- Ask open questions to find out more before moving to the solution

Stay focused

Practise active listening

Step 3. Reactions from you
Why are you giving feedback?
What might touch a nerve for you?
What has triggered your decision to give feedback now?
What outcome are you hoping for?
Detail the behaviour, incident, action, emotion behind the decision to give feedback
now

Double check by asking yourself:
Are you really giving feedback or are you asking, "Why aren't you like me?"

What dynamics are you contributing?
Take a few steps back: use the system lens

What kind of feedback is it?
Appreciation, steps, evaluation

Step 4. Moving the conversation forward
Keep it future focused
Put a follow-up process in place
Support around the learning circle

9

Implementation: being human

Hassan is at his wits end with a team member, Nadia. So much so that he has taken the drastic step of asking HR how he can close Nadia's contract on the grounds of her poor performance. They have responded frostily, telling him that he will have to "performance manage" Nadia before taking such action. They point out that there is no written evidence of poor performance from Nadia. In fact, there seems to be no evidence of any feedback whatsoever.

His boss, Gavin, is unsympathetic. Hassan has been going on about Nadia's limitations in their management meetings all year. How can there be nothing written down?

Hassan sulkily tries to explain that this is because Nadia derails all their feedback conversations, so they don't get very far.

"Well, get started now. Just say it," advises Gavin unhelpfully, fresh from a radical candour course.

So Hassan tries again. He calls a one-to-one meeting with Nadia. He decides to focus on Nadia's lack of writing skills and get her to rewrite a report. He carefully goes through the model he has learnt on his feedback course. He knows he is supposed to focus on specifics. He still struggles to tell Nadia exactly what is wrong with the report; it is completely not what he wanted.

However, he has gone through it and marked up some sections that could be worded differently. The feedback he is giving is the "steps and instruction" type of feedback mentioned earlier: "This is how to do it. First you do this, then you do this." It is more planned and careful than his usual meetings. He feels perhaps he is getting somewhere. He is proud of himself.

Then, halfway through the meeting, Nadia whips out her phone.

"I think it would be helpful for us to record this meeting, Hassan," she says. "So that I can go back to it and remind myself what to do. I mean, let's be honest, your instructions are not usually very clear. This is the first time you've bothered to show me what to do."

Hassan is appalled. He tells Nadia that recording all their meetings feels uncomfortable for him. He is offended that she thinks it's necessary. What is she up to? Does she want to sue him? He asks her to put her phone away so that they can continue with their meeting without it.

Nadia is horrified that he might think she wants to record the meeting for any other reason than her own learning, which she takes very seriously. She starts to cry and runs off to the toilets. Many people in the organisation rush to comfort her. Hassan feels like a monster. He blames himself for not being kinder to Nadia.

Gavin is summoned, as senior manager, to support his team. He has no idea what to do either. Reluctantly, he calls HR.

What next?

There is a lot going on in this scenario. Only some of the problems are due to the feedback itself.

This is often the case at work. Feedback, as we have discussed, can spark many emotional reactions, challenging both the person giving the feedback, as well as the person receiving the feedback. To begin with, it can trigger various sensitivities around people's relationship with their work.

It can then stray away from work and into wider identity stories. Nadia has many sensitivities around her career to date and her current role. She has struggled with various disabilities, and had to be creative in finding ways to get as far as she has. She is proud of what she has achieved. Hassan is shaking the foundations of her carefully planned approach to work, both by the haphazard way he runs his meetings and by suggesting she is wrong to use her tried and trusted technique of recording learning conversations.

Are your feedback conversations difficult?

Do some of your feedback conversations feel as difficult as Hassan and Nadia's? The specific complexities may vary. But however experienced you are, there will always be at least one discussion you dread. Bring it to mind, and we will look at how to deal with it shortly.

As you work through this chapter, you will find five key steps to follow, to make sure you get off to a flying start in dealing with your difficult discussions. We will build these into a checklist as we go along and you will be able to see the full checklist at the end of the chapter.

The five steps are these.

1. Start with yourself.
2. Challenge your beliefs, assumptions and biases.

3. Get outside your own head.

4. Understand the other person's emotions.

5. Consider neurodiversity.

What makes a discussion difficult?

You will have prepared carefully, interrogated your feedback data thoroughly, considered your own bias and limitations honestly, and spent hours anticipating every possible feedback conversation scenario.

Yet the conversation still feels impossible. The person you are giving feedback to always (you feel) derails the discussion, doesn't listen, doesn't want to learn, or perhaps is incapable of learning. You may be like Hassan, hoping HR will allow you to ask them to leave, or transfer them elsewhere. At the very least, you would prefer not to have to talk to this person ever again. At this point, you may want to drop the whole concept of giving feedback, thinking something like,

> "None of the models in this book work for me, because no one else in the entire world has ever had to deal with someone quite as complex and difficult as ... (Nadia, Hassan, Mateo, Antoine; you will have your own example). There is no point in me even *trying* to give them feedback. Conversations with them are always going to be too difficult."

As we have discussed, feedback puts people into that tense place where humans exist (i.e. they really want to learn and grow, but also have a desire to be accepted, loved and appreciated, exactly as they are.) As a result, an element of challenge will always be present when you discuss feedback. However, not all feedback conversations are equally difficult; for example, building on someone's excellent performance is likely to be a much easier conversation than tackling someone's issues with personal hygiene. So when a discussion feels difficult, it is important to explore what is going on.

Let's think a bit more about how you are defining your "difficult conversations".

Of course, each workplace adds a unique layer of issues to unpick, and organisational dynamics can be difficult to navigate. The Chartered Management Institute picks up on some key points:

> A difficult conversation is one whose primary subject matter is potentially contentious and/or sensitive and may elicit strong, complex emotions that can be hard to predict or control.[1]

You can see these dynamics played out in feedback conversations such as the Hassan/Nadia example, where you are conscious that there are all sorts of issues sloshing around. You are just not entirely sure what they are or what you should do with them.

This is because of the mass of confusing and conflicting **emotions** that lurk just under the surface of any difficult feedback conversation – your emotions, as well as the emotions of the person you are talking to.

They will wait there, until they are dredged up from the depths of your consciousness by the feedback you are trying to give. Then they will do their best to drag you down, so that you lose your way and your conversation feels impossible.

Why should you persevere, when it feels difficult?

By this stage in the book, you know how important good feedback is to support learning and growth. Giving feedback is not always easy. But none of the underlying issues get any easier if you ignore them. The more difficult it feels, the more important it probably is.

It may be helpful to know that you are not alone. There are Nadias, Mateos and Antoines (and your own named example) all over the place. Human beings are complex and human relationships are never completely straightforward.

The key point to consider here, in relation to feedback, is the importance of understanding more about the impact of sensitive/contentious subject matter and strong, complex emotions, both for you and the person you are giving feedback to. Better understanding will enable you to manage conversations that they might potentially derail.

How do you approach it?

When you dread a feedback discussion, the stages to work through are no different to when feedback feels ordinarily challenging. But you will have to dig deeper and do even more of all the important things we have been talking about throughout this book.

You know that giving good feedback will always mean being clear, prepared, helpful and human.

As you approach that difficult feedback discussion, you have to be:

- even clearer and even better prepared

- even more helpful
- even more human.

Fortunately, being even more human has its advantages. You can make it work for you, instead of letting it trip you up.

It is time to think a bit more about what this means in practical terms and move into the first step on our checklist.

Step 1. Start with yourself

Your key aim when giving feedback is to be helpful, using the giving good feedback framework.

But it is hard to be helpful when you are struggling to work out how you feel about the conversation. As a result, you will not always get your feedback conversations right first time. There will always be complications and difficulties, times when you wish you could go back and have that conversation again.

This is perfectly acceptable. You are human; therefore, you cannot be perfect and you are always learning.

Fortunately, the solution to difficult feedback discussions lies in that same humanity.

You are offering feedback to help someone else move round the learning circle. However, feedback is all about learning, both for the person you are offering it to and for you. In giving feedback to someone else, you will find out something new about yourself every time. You may not be able to have exactly the same conversation again, but you can review it, you can learn from it and next time you can do it better. You can make your humanity work for you.

Let's look at how you can get into the right headspace for the more difficult feedback meetings. The starting point is to learn more about yourself, and use this to inform your conversation planning. Bear in mind the following.

- The person you can influence most reliably is yourself.
- The emotions and reactions you can anticipate and control best are your own.
- It therefore makes sense to start your preparation and anticipation stages with yourself.

Ask yourself the following questions to help you surface whatever may be going on for you before you start the discussion.

- How do you feel about instigating the conversation?
- How do you feel about the issue/behaviour being discussed?
- How do you feel about the person you are talking to?

Be honest. As you consider each question, they will spark off a host of emotions. These emotions will be triggered by all the things you have going on, hidden in your psyche, under the surface of your feedback discussions.

Reviewing these questions should remind you to move to Step 2 on the checklist, which is to challenge various beliefs, assumptions and biases.

Step 2. Challenge your beliefs, assumptions and biases

If your feedback discussion is to be helpful, it will involve you moving from your view/interpretation of the behaviour you have observed to the other person's view/interpretation of their behaviour, all with the ultimate aim of reaching some kind of agreed approach for success. Being more in control of your emotions will help you manage this process.

Figure 8 shows the way the discussion should work.

However, when things feel difficult, you need to be more rigorous than usual in challenging your beliefs, assumptions and biases. It may be that the conversation feels difficult because it is bumping into, and getting stuck on, one of your biases or assumptions. If this happens, the conversation will not move round the circle and will not be helpful for the person you are giving feedback to.

It is never easy to be clear about your own biases and limitations. In Chapters 6 and 7, we looked at some techniques to help you explore the different things that might impact your

Figure 8. Helpful discussions

view of the situation and how to gain different perspectives on it. We also explored the impact of biases and background in some detail in Chapters 4 and 5. Here, we are focusing again on you and how you can "see yourself" better. In other words, you are going to get outside your own head. As you know very well by now, the best way to do this is to seek some feedback for yourself. You can therefore move on to Step 3 of our checklist.

Step 3. Get outside your own head

When a conversation gets stuck, due to your own particular bias, belief or assumption, you will be so focused on getting across your view that you will be unable to move into discussion mode. You will be trapped in the transmission mode that we discussed in Chapter 7.

As a result, you will not be able to move the conversation from your view or interpretation of the other person's behaviour to theirs. The discussion will therefore not be helpful. In fact, it will probably be downright difficult.

To get into the right headspace for a helpful discussion, seek some support and gain some distance from the way you feel about the conversation. Get outside your own head by talking the issue through with someone slightly distanced from the situation (this could be a mentor) or by talking out loud to yourself. It is rather like asking someone to watch the "film" we imagined in Chapter 7. This time, however, you are more interested in the scenes showing you and your reactions to the behaviour, rather than focusing on the behaviour of the person you are giving feedback to.

You can then ask your mentor or the mirror the questions in Question sheet 7 to check your preparation.

QUESTION SHEET 7. GET OUTSIDE YOUR OWN HEAD

Talk through the feedback you want to discuss

Talk it through as though *they* are the person you are giving feedback to

Can you explain coherently:
- why you need to have the conversation
- your view of the situation/interpretation of the behaviour
- what your feedback is
- what you hope to achieve from the conversation
- any of your own beliefs, assumptions or biases you have identified
- how might these trip you up?

How reasonable does this seem to them?
- What insights can the other person give about your beliefs, assumptions and biases?
- What have they noticed?
- What do they think might trip you up?
- What parts of the perceived difficulty do they think might be about you?
- What parts of it do they think you might have contributed to the situation?

Can they help you interrogate your feedback?
- Can you talk about the feedback from your own perspective?
- Or are you trying to pass on feedback from someone else that you haven't interrogated properly?
- Is it a one-off? Or do you have several examples of the behaviour that you want to talk about (not only from last week)?
- How are you describing the behaviour? Is it clear?

What else can you consider with them?
- Are there any neurodiverse issues?
- Do you need to bring in other help (e.g. HR)?
- Do you need to try different techniques when managing the person, to help them hear your feedback and move round the learning circle?
- Do you need to think about the language you use?

For example, "It's all sizzle and no steak" said one editor (looking at the uncomprehending vegetarian)

This process will help you interrogate the message you want to give, and plan the discussion so that it does not get mired in your beliefs, assumptions and biases. This should mean the discussion remains helpful and forward looking. Then you are better placed to move around the learning circle as you discuss the feedback and move from your view to the other person's view, and agree a way forward.

So far so good.

How are you feeling, now that your emotions are on the surface? Can they still trip you up? What about the other person? What's their perspective?

When giving feedback, it is also important to be aware that human beings do not generally find change easy. So if the person you are giving feedback to is going to take your feedback on board, learn from it and change their behaviour or actions, it will take some time and spark many emotions.

This can result in difficult discussions. Despite your careful feedback, and preparation focusing on yourself and your limitations, you can still be derailed by emotions. This time, however, by *the other person's emotions*.

Step 4. Understand the other person's emotions

As part of your preparation for difficult discussions, it is important to remember to give people time and space to process feedback and the associated emotions they might be feeling.

There are a variety of models that can help you consider and understand the emotions involved. Many are built on the Kübler-Ross bereavement curve, which describes the five common stages of grief.[2] Taken a step further, it can also be used to explore the emotions experienced during change.

This is because, when you experience change (i.e. do something new), you have to let go of whatever has gone before.

You therefore experience loss, on some level, even if whatever you are doing next is entirely positive. For example, if you become a millionaire and move to your dream house, you still have to say goodbye to the friends of your old neighbourhood and get used to a new routine. Of course, if the change is a negative one, the loss and the associated emotions can feel more acute.

The SARAH model

In the same way, if you receive feedback that you do not expect or that conflicts with your own ideas about your performance, you will need some time to let go of your own view before you can move to thinking differently.

The SARAH model takes the Kübler-Ross model and produces a version specifically aimed at helping people understand how a recipient of feedback might react, and the support that might be needed at each stage, as shown in Figure 9 on the next page.

It follows the idea that there are five stages that people may need to go through before they can take feedback on board, learn from it and do anything useful with it.

S is for shock. People need time to absorb and process what you're saying in private. You might want to have an initial conversation and then suggest another meeting another day.

A is for anger. People may seem to take it on board initially but then get angry and want to argue. This is part of the process.

R is for resistance. People may want to be defensive, reject your feedback, decide it is not their fault. People can get very stuck at this point. It is important to provide facts and information and to reinforce that your goal is to work together to find a way forward.

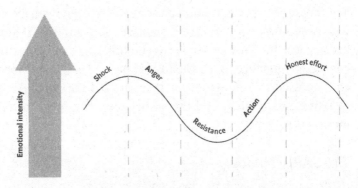

Figure 9. The SARAH model

A is for action. This is when action can start to happen, and people can plan and build strategies. There may need to be some back and forth here.

H is for honest effort. Change takes time. Nothing happens overnight and even if feedback is accepted, old habits die hard. Encourage the honest effort and give people time. This is where a lot of organisations fall down.

Rushing people through these stages is where your feedback discussions are likely to get derailed or stuck.

Try working through this model, using the example person you have been considering in the last two chapters. Bring to mind a feedback discussion with them which you felt did not go well. Can you pinpoint where, in this model, it might have come to a halt?

We can use the Hassan/Nadia scenario as an example and work through it, using SARAH.

S is for shock

People need time to absorb and process what you're saying in private. You might want to have an initial conversation and then suggest another meeting another day.

Nadia is taken by surprise when Hassan starts giving her feedback. He seems suddenly to be raising a lot of points about her performance – in her view, from nowhere. She has previously tried to talk to him about giving her information in a particular way, but he hasn't listened. He is speaking more loudly and she is finding it hard to listen to him.

She thinks perhaps recording the meeting will help her. But he shouts about this too. She can't believe what she is hearing.

When Hassan is stressed, he tends to raise his voice and sound aggressive. He is appalled when she whips out her phone and suggests the recording. He is sure Nadia is setting him up for some kind of tribunal. HR might listen to it. Nadia could post it on the internet. Anything!

At this point, Hassan could draw the meeting to a halt.

"Nadia, I can see that I have given you a lot of new information here, and you have also given me something to think about. Can we stop so that we both have time to process this? We can talk again tomorrow."

A is for anger

People may seem to take it on board initially but then get angry and want to argue. This is part of the process.

Nadia is mortified that Hassan seems to be suggesting her intentions in recording the meeting are sinister. Initially she apologises; she feels terrible. Then she thinks that Hassan is the one being unreasonable. She starts to argue, Hassan shouts back, she runs off to the toilets in tears.

Many people in the organisation rush to comfort her.

Hassan meanwhile is reeling. He was ready (he is sure) to be helpful and supportive and Nadia has ruined it right from the start. Like she always does. What can he do?

Letting people make their points and responding calmly is important. When people are angry, it is helpful to take a pause so that they can gather themselves.

"I really want to hear your points and discuss them. Just now, I can see that you are feeling angry and upset. Shall we take a break?"

Going back to the listening model in the last chapter will be useful.

"Nadia, I can see that you feel strongly about this. Let me just make sure I have got your points correct, I think I heard you saying ... Have I understood you properly? Is that the right summary of the issues you have raised?"

R is for resistance

People may want to be defensive, reject your feedback, decide it is not their fault. People can get very stuck at this point. It is important to provide facts and information and to reinforce that your goal is to work together to find a way forward.

Nadia decides this is another example of Hassan's unhelpful, erratic behaviour, the behaviour she keeps trying to give him feedback about, though he never listens. She feels vindicated now in everything she has said about him. She goes home for the day.

Hassan is torn between blaming himself and thinking the

way she is behaving is a complete vindication of his original request to HR – to close her contract. Gavin is summoned, as senior manager, to support his team. He has no idea what to do either. Reluctantly he calls HR.

Once you have taken a break to let people calm down, you can go back and address their points. If you have interrogated your data well, you will be able to use this to make the discussion helpful at this point.

"I'd like to take the time to explore both points in some detail before we move to looking at any solutions. Let's start with ... Let's talk about this particular report. This is what I have noticed ..."

In working together to find a way forward, you may need to seek other support/involve other departments, for example HR.

A is for action

This is when action can start to happen, and people can plan and build strategies. There may need to be some back and forth here.

HR have long conversations with Hassan and Nadia (and Gavin, but that is another story). They suggest looking at some of the issues with neurodiversity and arrange some further support. Specifically, they also run a facilitated meeting between Hassan and Nadia and arrange an occupational assessment for them both, so that they can discuss the neurodiverse issues they both have to deal with. Nadia starts to feel she is being heard.

Reluctantly she starts to decide that perhaps Hassan may have one or two reasonable points.

"Perhaps I shouldn't just argue and throw everything back into Hassan's face," she says.

Hassan begins to realise what he has contributed to the situation and feels a little less isolated now that some of his issues have been recognised. He breathes a sigh of relief.

"Perhaps I can try some of Nadia's ways of remembering things," he says, agreeing to the recording idea.

Recording their discussions means he has to prepare; this is a good discipline for him. It helps diffuse the emotions. Because there is something for them both to refer back to, there is no disagreement about what has been said.

It also gives them both feedback they cannot argue with as it presents the conversation back, at a distance, without comment. As a result, it is easier for each of them to see what was helpful or unhelpful about their approach.

At this point, you are helping the person bridge the gap between their view and yours so that you can move forward. As part of your back and forth, going back to your clear data, building on it with anything useful the person has raised and then moving to alternative action will keep this focused on the future.

"Nadia, we've discussed the report in some detail, and we're looking at what you need to do differently to match it to this report template in future. You've expressed concerns about what exactly you have to do. Tell me more about that? How can I help?

H is for honest effort

Change takes time. Nothing happens overnight and even if feedback is accepted, old habits die hard. Encourage the honest effort and give people time. This is where a lot of organisations fall down.

It takes a while. There are more meetings at which HR have to be involved. Hassan and Nadia both need some individual support, and the first time Nadia tries to implement the feedback, she falls flat on her face. But they keep trying and they get there. After a fashion. They are still the same people. They are just learning new behaviours at work.

Putting in place a process for follow-up is important, such as regular catch-ups, a specific objective to review, a timescale. This will help applaud the effort and keep progress on track.

"So we have agreed ... Let's meet again in a month to review how things are going on XYZ."

Could this have been easier?

This meeting did not have to be so difficult. We can look at the last step of our checklist to think about what could have made it all easier.

Step 5. Consider neurodiversity

A learning point from the SARAH model is that when things feel difficult, it is worth treating them like the proverbial enemy. "Keep your friends close, but your enemies closer."

When discussions feel difficult, they need more time and attention, not less. The more they are put off and ignored, the harder they get.

Feedback is always about two people. Feedback always says as much (usually more) about the feedback giver as it does about the person receiving the feedback. As we discussed in Chapter 8, feedback does not always land as you expect.

However, it can also be helpful to consider neurodiversity

and the way that different neurodiverse conditions can affect the way people learn and hear feedback.[3]

Nadia's sudden request to record the meeting was a shock to Hassan. However, for her it was sensible process that she had developed to deal with issues she had around retaining and processing information.

Regular discussions using specific, carefully interrogated examples of behaviour using the PACES model would have meant Hassan was not taken by surprise by this request.

These meetings would still have felt difficult but would have helped Hassan pick up on Nadia's struggles earlier. At this point, he could have discussed ways in which he could help her retain and process information. He could also have sought some support for her neurodiverse issues and looked at other ways to support Nadia hear the feedback. This would have helped Nadia become better equipped, over time, to hear the feedback and feel more cared for.

As Hassan prepared for these meetings, he would also have been able to explore some of his own issues and develop a greater understanding of them. This might have helped him guard against overreacting when he felt Nadia was challenging him.

If, for example, he had noticed that Nadia had not done some of the work he had asked her to do, he could have discussed this, working through his PACES.

- I've put you in charge of stage three for the project we are working on.
- The deadline was three weeks ago. I've noticed this still hasn't been completed.

- This is causing a problem for me because we need to stay on track to complete the project.
- What's your take on that?
- What can I do to help?

The last two questions would have put them in a more constructive space and enabled them to move forward. They could then have agreed a joint plan of action.

Gavin, as part of his regular follow-ups, could have spotted Hassan's rather haphazard approach to work. He could have held regular discussions with Hassan about his management of Nadia and what he was doing to support her. Gavin then might have noticed Hassan's tendency to get distracted and not focus on one job at a time.

If he had asked "What can I do to help?", they could have reviewed some techniques to help Hassan organise his approach to tasks or even external support to help him manage a difficult situation.[4]

If you have a neurodiverse condition

If you have a neurodiverse condition, it can be helpful to take control and manage the feedback you get up front. Most people want to do the right thing and most organisations will have policies to support any adjustments required to meet different needs.

Take the time to tell your manager or your colleagues what is going on for you and what would be helpful. Believe me, they are probably feeling insecure and worried about what to do, so they will be grateful for you taking the initiative.

If it is not in place already, introduce them to the idea of wellness action plans, mentioned in Chapter 6, which cover what they can do to help you keep well and support you in doing your best work for the organisation. You can then use these to consider what you can put in place *together*. Once a plan is in place, it will be easier to feedback on how it is working and any changes needed.

You are now well placed to be able to handle any type of feedback discussion. The steps to follow when preparing for a difficult discussion are detailed in Checklist 3.

Difficult conversations are part of life at work. You can run, but you can't hide. The more you try to run away, the more difficult the conversations will get.

You have the resources now. Embrace those difficult discussions, don't put them off.

Before you get started, just make sure that you are:

- even more clear
- even more prepared
- even more human

than you ever thought was necessary or even possible.

CHECKLIST 3. IMPLEMENTATION: BEING HUMAN

Step 1. Start with yourself

Consider the emotions you are experiencing as you contemplate this difficult conversation

- How do you feel about instigating the conversation?
- How do you feel about the issue/behaviour being discussed?
- How do you feel about the person involved?
- Being more in control of your emotions will help you manage the conversation

Step 2. Challenge your beliefs, assumptions and biases
Work through your meeting plan. Can you move from:
- your own view/interpretation of the observed behaviour
- to the other person's interpretation/view of the issue
- with the aim of reaching some kind of agreed approach for success?

Where is the conversation likely to get stuck?
What beliefs, assumptions and biases is it likely to bump against?

Step 3. Get outside your own head
Plan your discussion with someone distanced from the situation
- How reasonable does the feedback seem to them?
- What insights can they give about your own beliefs, assumptions and biases?
- What have they noticed?
- What do they think might trip you up?

What parts of the perceived difficulty do they think might be about you and what you have contributed to the situation?

Can they help you interrogate your feedback?

Step 4. Understand the emotions
Work through the SARAH model

S is for shock. People need time to absorb and process what you're saying in private. You might want to have an initial conversation and then suggest another meeting another day

A is for anger. People may seem to take it on board initially but then get angry and want to argue. This is part of the process

R is for rejection. People may want to be defensive, reject your feedback, decide it is not their fault. People can get very stuck at this point. It is important to provide facts and information and to reinforce that your goal is to work together to find a way forward

A is for action. This is when action can start to happen, and people can plan and build strategies. There may need to be some back and forth here

H is for honest effort. Change takes time. Nothing happens overnight and even if feedback is accepted, old habits die hard. Encourage the honest effort and give people time. This is where a lot of organisations fall down

Step 5. Consider neurodiversity
Don't expect to get it right first time
When things feel difficult, they need more time and attention, not less. The more they are put off and ignored, the harder they get
- Do you need to access some further support?
- Have you considered the appropriate language?

Epilogue: Six golden rules for giving good feedback

And so here we are at the end of the book. Well done for working your way through it. You should now have a host of tools at your disposal to help you give good feedback at work, at home and anywhere else you choose.

If you are still feeling a bit like the Four Horsemen of the Apocalypse at the beginning of the book, remember that all good horsemen have back-up forces to call on when they need them.

Now that you have read this book, you have back-up forces too. Remember all the different points we have covered about what is involved in giving good feedback.

In the first place, feedback is all about communication. In a simple communication loop, it shows that your message has been received and understood.

Giving and receiving feedback will always have its challenges. The challenges come from our status as humans: we want to belong and we want people to like us. This can make it hard both to offer feedback ("What if I upset them?") and to receive it ("Why don't you love me just the way I am?").

Giving good feedback will always involve:

- being clear and prepared
- being helpful
- being human.

We will not always get it right first time. This is because we are human; therefore, we cannot be perfect.

But fortunately, as humans, we also have a desire to learn and grow. We may not be able to have exactly the same conversation again, but we can review it, we can learn from it and next time we can do it better. This is as it should be – feedback is all about moving round the learning circle.

Feel the forces

As a handy guide, keep your FORCES available to remind you how to do it well. Figure 10 shows the six forces that lead to good feedback.

So off you go. Get on and give good feedback. Just say it!

But make sure you work though the appropriate checklist first.

Have you thought of everything?

You can use Checklist 4 to remind you of all the useful feedback forces you have available to you.

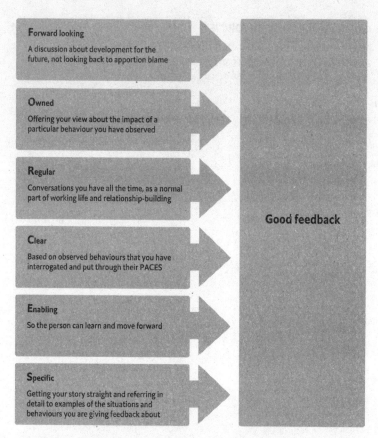

Forward looking

A discussion about development for the future, not looking back to apportion blame

Owned

Offering your view about the impact of a particular behaviour you have observed

Regular

Conversations you have all the time, as a normal part of working life and relationship-building

Clear

Based on observed behaviours that you have interrogated and put through their PACES

Enabling

So the person can learn and move forward

Specific

Getting your story straight and referring in detail to examples of the situations and behaviours you are giving feedback about

Good feedback

Figure 10. FORCES: the six golden rules for giving good feedback

CHECKLIST 4. FEEDBACK FORCES

Forward looking Look forwards about development for the future, not backwards to apportion blame	**Keep it future focused** (Chapter 8) • Why are you giving feedback? • What outcome are you hoping for? **Discuss, don't transmit** (Chapter 8) Explain and Explore Share for Success
Owned Offer your view or reaction to a particular behaviour you have observed and the impact of this on you, the team and the work you are producing together	**Use the giving good feedback framework** (Chapter 1) • Remember you are offering information about your opinions on and reactions to the behaviour, and its impact on you, the work or the team • You are not offering a universal, agreed truth **Start with yourself** (Chapter 9) Understand your own emotions as you contemplate this conversation Feedback is always about two people and says more about the giver than the receiver (Chapters 4 and 8) **Consider what dynamics you are contributing** (Chapters 4, 5 and 8) Take a step back; use the system lens (Chapter 8)
Regular Conversations you have all the time, as a normal part of working life	**Put effort into building your relationships at work** (Chapters 6, 7 and 8) • Regular 1–1 meetings and chats with your team • Avoid unhelpful, reinforcing communication loops (Chapter 4) • Diffuse a difficult relationship by thinking about the part each of you plays and what each of you is contributing to the problem (Chapter 4)

	Plan your feedback process and follow-up (Chapter 7) • Write down your feedback • Review your feedback data from a broader perspective (patterns/themes)
	Lead by example (Chapter 6) • Offer regular opportunities to share feedback as a team (e.g. "Ta-dahs!") • Ask others for specific examples and the impact of your behaviour (e.g. "What one thing can I do?") • Consider how your approach to feedback is impacted by organisational culture
	Consider neurodiversity (Chapters 6 and 9) • When things feel difficult, they need more time and attention, not less • Do you need to access some further support?
Clear Take people constructively through helpful examples	**Gather your feedback data** **Put your feedback data through its PACES** (Chapter 7)
Enabling So the person can learn and move forward	**What is their perspective?** **What did you do and say during the specific example?** • Use your listening skills to explore (Chapter 8) • Use the SARAH model (Chapter 9)
Specific Refer in detail to examples of the situations and behaviours you are giving feedback about	**Interrogate your feedback data** (Chapter 7) **Check your bias** (Chapters 4, 5 and 7) • Review your film script (Chapter 7) • Consider what you have contributed to this dynamic • Are you really giving feedback? Or are you asking, "Why aren't you more like me?"

Acknowledgements

It starts with a story. Of course it does. Everything to do with feedback starts with a story.

Over the years, a variety of people have landed in my office, to share their daily stories and seek help in dealing with the general trials and tribulations of being at work. Giving or receiving feedback formed a big part of these discussions and stories ranged from the good and the bad to the downright ugly. Generally, though, people just wanted support to do their best, learn from mistakes and do better next time.

Consequently, in my professional life, I've tried out hundreds of different techniques, strategies, models and approaches in a bid to help people navigate organisational life and use feedback to learn and grow.

This book aims to share some of the learning from those experiences, so a big thank you to everyone for offering helpful feedback to let me know what worked and what didn't work at the time. (Of course, some experiments in learning methods worked better than others. I can only apologise to the unfortunate people who had to sit through the less useful ones.)

And thanks to all the Dark Angels and "26" members for feedback and support, Gemma Blencowe and Lee Ryan for ideas and Jem Stein for the introduction.

I have already dedicated the book to Steve. But since he has been so positive and supportive throughout the writing process (providing ideas as well as doing a lot of cooking), I'll mention him again, along with Amy, Sophie and Rosie, who have been gratifyingly impressed that they could pre-order a book by their mother on Amazon, and Liz, who is willing to jet off to various airport shops and demand the book be ordered instantly.

Finally, thanks to any other family members, friends and acquaintances who have responded to news of the book, with variations on: "You're writing a book about feedback? That's going to be really useful. The problem I have with feedback is ..."

I hope the result answers these issues for you.

Notes

Part 1: What is feedback and why does it matter?

Chapter 1: What is feedback?

1. "Feedback is the breakfast of champions". Ken Blanchard (author of *The One Minute Manager*, 1982) attributes this saying to Rick Tate, a former consulting partner in his company (Ken Blanchard blog, August 17th 2009). He also makes the point that not all jobs offer immediate feedback via sales or numbers, so it's good to hear from other people.

2. David Kolb, *Experiential Learning: Experience as the Source of Learning and Development* (New Jersey: Pearson, 1983).

3. With thanks to David Kolb and Experience Based Learning Systems, LLC, for permission to reproduce Figure 2.5 from *Experiential Learning: Experience as the Source of Learning and Development* (second edition).

4. In their book *Nine Lies about Work: A Freethinking Leader's Guide to the Real World* (Cambridge, MA: Harvard, 2019), Marcus Buckingham and Ashley Goodall write scathingly about the reliance of organisations on competency models. They talk about the danger of us accepting unpopular systems at work as universal "settled truths". The authors contend that they are nothing of the sort, describing many corporate processes such as competency models, where feedback is given in relation to a pre-defined set of criteria, as "mind numbing and damaging".

5. A system where feedback is gathered not just from people more senior than you but also from colleagues and more junior workers, and then collated, and presented to you in the form of a report.

These systems are often treated as confidential, to encourage people to contribute feedback, so the feedback is often anonymous.

6. Buckingham and Goodall are joined in their criticisms by others commenting on the limitations of most organisational appraisal systems. For example, Lucy Kellaway, writing about her own experiences of appraisals, describes them as a random mix of praise and criticism, referring to events that are too long ago to remember, immortalised in a long and complex form and kept, alarmingly, on a file. If you are unlucky, they also incorporate a damning, one-word summary describing your overall performance, such as "underachieving". L. Kellaway, "It's time to sack job appraisals", *Financial Times*, July 11th 2010.

7. Aristotle was an ancient Greek philosopher and polymath during the Classical period in ancient Greece. Taught by Plato, he was the founder of the Peripatetic school of philosophy within the Lyceum and the wider Aristotelean tradition. His model of communication is speaker-centred, i.e. the speaker has the central role and is the only one who is active.

8. David Berlo published his source–message–channel–receiver model in his book *The Process of Communication: Introduction to Theory and Practice* (New York: Holt, Rinehart & Winston, 1960).

9. Model developed thanks to a training course at Roffey Park Institute (www.roffeypark.ac.uk) many years ago, which introduced me to the concept of feedback on observed behaviours (the outer circle) rather than on personality, sense of self or values (the inner circle).

Chapter 2: Why does feedback matter?

1. M. Buckingham and A. Goodall, *Nine Lies about Work: A Freethinking Leader's Guide to the Real World* (Cambridge, MA: Harvard, 2019).

2. B. Wigert and J. Harter, "Re-engineering performance management", Gallup (2017).

3. J. Zenger and J. Folkman, "Why do so many managers avoid giving praise?", *Harvard Business Review* (May 2017).

4. Buckingham and Goodall debate this in *Nine Lies about Work*. They posit that millennials actually want the opposite, a workplace where

there is no feedback but lots of uncritical attention, similar to the attention received from social media sites such as Snapchat.

5. David Rock, co-founder of the NeuroLeadership Institute, comments on the effect that feedback has on us (i.e. similar to footsteps behind us on a dark night), and explores the impact of this in detail. D. Rock, "SCARF: a brain-based model for collaborating with and influencing others", *NeuroLeadership Journal*, 1 (2008).

6. D. Stone and S. Heen, *Thanks for the Feedback: The Science and Art of Receiving Feedback Well, Even When It Is Off Base, Unfair, Poorly Delivered, and, Frankly, You're Not In The Mood* (New York: Penguin, 2015). Their view is that we all spend too much time "wrong spotting" (i.e. finding fault with feedback that we don't agree with), rather than trying to make use of the feedback. We also use other people's limitations as an excuse for not communicating well ourselves. They suggest we can all grow and develop more effectively if we focus on learning more about ourselves and our own barriers to good communication. If we put some work into overcoming these barriers, we will be able to make use of feedback, however hopelessly unskilled the person offering it may be. Blind spots are a case in point; feedback about these helps us see things we otherwise would not.

7. The Dunning–Kruger effect is a cognitive bias that posits that when people are unskilled in a particular area, they are far more likely to overestimate their competence in that area. Some researchers also include in their definition the opposite effect for high performers – their tendency to underestimate their skills.

8. Ray Dalio, in his book *Principles: Life and Work* (New York: Simon & Schuster, 2017), outlines his faith in the idea of radical transparency. This led to a range of brutal experiments in some companies, which encouraged harsh feedback and subjected workers to intense and awkward real-time 360s.

9. M. Buckingham and A. Goodall, "The feedback fallacy", *Harvard Business Review* (March–April 2019). Their starting point is that feedback does the opposite of helping people to learn. Telling people what we think of their performance doesn't help them thrive and

excel, and telling people how we think they should improve actually hinders learning.

10. K. Scott, *Radical Candor: Be a Kick-Ass Boss Without Losing Your Humanity* (New York: St Martin's Press, 2017). Kim Scott labels behaviour from unpleasant bosses (all challenge and no care) as "obnoxious aggression" and suggests, when faced with it, that the best thing to do is just quietly locate the nearest exit. She describes this approach as "challenge directly and care personally".

11. Stone and Heen, *Thanks for the Feedback.*

12. Figure 3 reproduced from "The Radical Candor Framework" from "Preface to the Revised Edition" in *Radical Candor: Be a Kick-Ass Boss Without Losing Your Humanity*, fully revised and updated edition by Kim Scott, copyright © 2019 by Kim Scott. Reprinted by permission of St. Martin's Press, New York. All rights reserved.

13. Tasha Eurich develops this idea and reviews different studies in her book *Insight: The Surprising Truth About How Others See Us, How We See Ourselves, and Why the Answers Matter More Than We Think* (NSW, Australia: Currency, 2018). One study suggests that 95% of us think we have strong self-awareness, but only about 10–15% of us actually possess it.

Chapter 3: What makes feedback good?

1. John Stuart Mill, *On Liberty* (London: Parker & Son, 1859).

2. Stone and Heen, *Thanks for the Feedback.*

3. Training sessions, drawing on ideas from Alan H. Palmer's book *Talk Lean: Shorter Meetings. Quicker Results. Better Relations* (Mankato, MN: Capstone, 2013).

4. Ray Dalio, *Principles: Life and Work.*

5. M. Heffernan "Why it's time to forget the pecking order at work", TEDTalk (2015). Margaret Heffernan recounts the tale of experiments (the Muir superchicken research).

6. R. C. Schank, *Tell Me a Story: Narrative and Intelligence* (Evanston, IL: Northwestern University Press, 1995).

7. For example, see Nicole Schneider's blog on "NLP Internal and External Reference", Global NLP Training (April 1st 2020). The

discipline of neurolinguistic programming suggests that people have different frames of reference – some people are very internally referenced and others are externally referenced. This means that some people need lots of feedback from others to know how they are doing; other people work it out for themselves.

Part 2: What gets in the way?

Chapter 4: Personal experience and style

1. See Quentin Crisp's autobiography *The Naked Civil Servant* (London: Penguin, 1968).
2. The Myers–Briggs Type Indicator is a questionnaire indicating different preferences in how people see the world and make decisions. It was developed by Katherine Cook Briggs and Isabel Briggs Myers and inspired by Carl Jung's book *Psychological Types*.
3. To borrow an analogy that David Foster Wallace used in his "This Is Water" commencement speech in 2005, talking about freedom rather than feedback when we are initially forced to peer out of the "tiny, skull-sized kingdoms" of which we are lords.
4. In *Thanks for the Feedback*, Stone and Heen talk about "wrong spotting". Blind spots are things other people can see that we can't. This is useful, though if we are wrong spotting, we dismiss them.
5. Neuroscience looks at what we watch and look for. For example, in an interview on *Science Friday* neuroscientist Sophie Scott of University College London talks about our speech-to-speech voice, i.e. our own voice that we are unable to hear ("How does the brain decode speech?", NPR, May 29th 2009). Science writer Steven Johnson talks about how we measure other people's moods by watching the corner of their mouths or scanning their eyes, without really being aware of what we are doing, in his book *Mind Wide Open: Your Brain and the Neuroscience of Everyday Life* (New York: Simon & Schuster, 2004).
6. Stone and Heen, *Thanks for the Feedback*.
7. You can read more about this in this article by Hannah Booth: "What I've learned from 10 years of therapy – and why it's time to stop", *Guardian*, April 30th 2022.

8. Stone and Heen, *Thanks for the Feedback*.
9. C. S. Dweck, *Mindset: The New Psychology of Success* (New York: Random House, 2006).
10. C. S. Dweck, "Brainology: transforming students' motivation to learn", Stanford Growth Mindset (2008).
11. V. Job, K. Bernecker and C. S. Dweck, "Are implicit motives the need to feel certain affect? Motive–affect congruence predicts relationship satisfaction", *Personality and Social Psychology Bulletin*, 38(12) (2012).
12. M. Ivanov and P. D. Werner, "Behavioural communication: individual differences in communication style", *Personality and Individual Differences*, 49(1) (2010).
13. Quiet quitting: an informal term, recently popularised, to denote reducing the number of tasks you complete at work without any discussion with a manager or employer.

Chapter 5: Bias

1. R. Dobelli, *The Art of Thinking Clearly: Better Thinking, Better Decisions* (London: Sceptre, 2014).
2. D. Rynders, "Battling implicit bias in the IDEA to advocate for African American students with disabilities", *Touro Law Review*, 35(1) (2019).
3. Studies of gender and leadership have found not only that women are considered less favourably than men for leadership positions, but also that if women do display the qualities considered important for leadership, these qualities are considered less favourably than when demonstrated by a man. A. H. Eagly and S. J. Karau, "Role congruity theory of prejudice toward female leaders", *Psychological Review*, 109(3) (2002).
    Minorities can face a double prejudice if they demonstrate behaviours not typically associated with their group, which can be responded to negatively.
4. This theory is expounded in K. Bezrukova et al., "A meta-analytical integration of over 40 years of research on diversity training evaluation", *Psychological Bulletin*, 142(11) (2016).
5. Research by Stacey Sinclair and others suggests that parental racial attitudes can influence children's implicit prejudice. S. Sinclair, E.

Dunn and B. S. Lowery, "The relationship between parental racial attitudes and children's implicit prejudice", *Journal of Experimental Social Psychology*, 41(3) (2005).

Parents are not the only figures who can influence such attitudes. Siblings, the school setting and the culture in which you grow up can also play a role.

Research by Frances Aboud and colleagues at McGill University in 1973 suggested that, even before kindergarten, children have already begun to seek out patterns and recognise what distinguishes them from other groups. They use their group membership (e.g. their racial group, gender group, age group) to guide their ideas about other people's psychological and behavioural traits. This process of recognising what sets you apart from others, and then forming negative opinions about outgroups (i.e. social groups with which an individual does not identify) contributes to the development of implicit biases. F. E. Aboud, D. M. Taylor and R. G. Doumani, "The effect of contact on the use of role and ethnic stereotypes in person perception", *Journal of Social Psychology*, 89(2) (1973).

6. Research by Glick and Fiske in 1996 on gender stereotypes explored perceptions of women. P. Glick and S. T. Fiske, "The ambivalent sexism inventory: differentiating hostile and benevolent sexism", *Journal of Personality and Social Psychology*, 70(3) (1996).

For example, looking at the way women can be viewed along a spectrum that varies from warm, nurturing and needing protection to hard and competitive, with "queen bees" provoking either benevolent or hostile forms of prejudice in turn. Hillary Clinton was a good example of this sort of bias when running against Donald Trump. Frequent gendered criticisms included comments that her voice was too loud or annoying; commentary on her choice of dress (with some people recommending that she only wear dark colours, and others saying she should wear colours "to look more cheerful"); and advice that she look at a picture of her granddaughter when speaking to prevent her from "looking so angry".

7. Buckingham and Goodall review this idea in *Nine Lies about Work*.

8. You can find confirmation of this theory by watching repeat episodes of the British TV series *Midsomer Murders*. Here, there is at least one murder in a quiet, country village every week, as a result of seething emotions from seemingly minor issues, such as decisions made at country shows. Nobody appears to find this odd; the villagers clearly have a good understanding of the power and devastation that can be caused by making decisions based on flawed data.

9. Research by Scullen, Mount and Goff, looking at the way each rater chose a rating, concluded that the only way it could be explained was the unique personality of the rater. The ratings revealed more about the rater than they did about the person being rated, thus making the ratings mirrors rather than tools. S. E. Scullen, M. K. Mount and M. Goff, "Understanding the latent structure of job performance ratings", *Journal of Applied Psychology*, 85 (2000).

10. Researchers have developed various tests to help them reveal implicit bias. For example, the Implicit Association Test (IAT) gets participants to categorise negative and positive words together with either images or words. Tests are taken online and must be performed as quickly as possible; the faster you categorise certain words or faces of a category, the stronger the bias you hold about that category. For example, the race IAT requires participants to categorise white faces and black faces and negative and positive words. The relative speed of association of black faces with negative words is used as an indication of the level of racist bias.

11. Learning about other cultures or outgroups and what language and behaviours they may find offensive is critical too. Researchers in Madison, Wisconsin designed a videogame called "Fair Play" in which players assume the role of a black graduate student named Jamal Davis. As Jamal, players experience subtle race bias while completing quests to obtain a science degree. The researchers hypothesised that participants who were randomly assigned to play the game would have greater empathy for Jamal and lower implicit race bias than participants randomised to read narrative text (not perspective taking) describing Jamal's experience. This hypothesis

was supported, illustrating the benefits of perspective taking in increasing empathy. B. Gutierrez et al., "'Fair Play': a videogame designed to address implicit race bias through active perspective taking", *Games for Health Journal*, 3(6) (2014).

12. A. G. Greenwald, M. R. Banaji and B. A. Nosek, "Statistically small effects of the Implicit Association Test can have societally large effects", *Journal of Personality and Social Psychology*, 108(4) (2015). A. G. Greenwald, et al., "Understanding and using the Implicit Association Test: III. Meta-analysis of predictive validity", *Journal of Personality and Social Psychology*, 97(1) (2009). F. L. Oswald et al., "Predicting ethnic and racial discrimination: a meta-analysis of IAT criterion studies", *Journal of Personality and Social Psychology*, 105(2) (2013).

13. A 2016 study found that brief meditation decreased unconscious bias against black people and elderly people, providing initial insight into the usefulness of this approach and paving the way for future research on this intervention. A. Lueke and B. Gibson, "Brief mindfulness meditation reduces discrimination", *Psychology of Consciousness: Theory, Research, and Practice*, 3(1) (2016).

14. Charlie Munger, partner of Warren Buffett, described the effect of several biases coming together as a "lollapalooza", which is where many biases together have a large-scale impact on human behaviour. Sometimes they are negative and nonsensical, and sometimes (e.g. in the case of the Alcoholics Anonymous model) there is a positive outcome. The term "lollapalooza" has since become part of investment jargon. C. Munger, "The psychology of human misjudgment", speech delivered at Harvard University (1995).

15. Buckingham and Goodall, *Nine Lies about Work*.

16. Sociologists have developed various theories around labelling and the impact it has. Howard Saul Becker's book *Outsiders: Studies in the Sociology of Deviance* (Glencoe, IL: Free Press, 1963) was extremely influential in the development of labelling theory and the rise to popularity of this theory. There have been many studies since then, looking at the impact of labels in the way that teachers treat students, such as Rosenthal and Jacobson's study in 1968

and Margaret Fuller's study of black girls in a London school. R. Rosenthal and L. Jacobson, "Pygmalion in the classroom", *Urban Review*, 3 (1968). M. Fuller, "Black girls in a London comprehensive school", in Martyn Hammersley and Peter Woods (eds), *Life in School: The Sociology of Pupil Culture* (Abingdon: Routledge, 1984).

Erving Goffman, president of the American Sociological Association, built on this, and is one of the United States' most cited sociologists. His most popular books include *The Presentation of Self in Everyday Life* (New York, Doubleday, 1956), *Interaction Ritual: Essays on Face-to-Face Behaviour* (New York: Pantheon, 1967), and *Frame Analysis* (New York: Harper & Row, 1974).

Chapter 6: Organisational culture

1. E. Burke, *The Speeches of the Right Honourable Edmund Burke in the House of Commons and Westminster Hall* (London: Longman, 1816).
2. Goffman, *Presentation of Self*.
3. Amy Edmondson has recently developed theories around this in her book *The Fearless Organisation: Creating Psychological Safety in the Workplace for Learning, Innovation, and Growth* (Hoboken, NJ: Wiley, 2018).
4. R. Cross, R. Rebele and A. Grant, "Collaborative overload", *Harvard Business Review* (January–February 2016).
5. E.H. Schein and W. G. Bennis, *Personal and Organizational Change Through Group Methods* (Hoboken, NJ: Wiley, 1965). This book first introduced the term "psychological safety" as a catalyst for organisational change. Schein and Bennis built on Lewin's three-stage model of organisational learning and change by suggesting that psychologically safe work environments facilitate the unfreezing process where employees become perceptive to changes in the status quo.
6. Edmondson, *Fearless Organization*. The person in charge and the environment they create can play a large part. Caroline F. Zink et al. look at the neural mechanisms that process social superiority and inferiority in humans, where social hierarchies can be established along various dimensions. C. F. Zink et al., "Know your place: neural processing of social hierarchy in humans", *Neuron*, 58(2) (2008).

7. Daniel Goleman, Richard Boyatzis and Annie McGee identify six emotional leadership styles in their book *Primal Leadership: Realizing the Power of Emotional Intelligence* (Cambridge, MA: Harvard Business School, 2002).

8. See the article by Richard Claydon of EQ Lab: "Why we need dependable, not radical, candor", EQLab, June 15th 2021. Claydon comments that, culturally, it is worth being aware that many of the leadership style traits that inform textbooks today are the same traits displayed by alpha males in a North American cultural context – assertive, self-confident and comfortable asserting their rightness in presentations, meetings and when giving feedback. This is because much of the leadership research was carried out on subjects who were predominantly white, North American men. However these traits are not always the most useful.

9. Ed Schein explores this further in his book *Humble Inquiry:* E. H. Schein and P. A. Schein, *Humble Inquiry: The Gentle Art of Asking Instead of Telling* (Oakland, CA: Berrett-Koehler, 2013).

   You can read a profile of Eileen Fisher in the Huffington Post. M. Tenney, "Be a 'don't knower': one of Eileen Fisher's secrets to success", HuffPost (May 15th 2015). In this profile, Tenney writes about Fisher's modelling of vulnerability and humility as a leader, which helps create psychological safety. Fisher expounds on her approach: "When you don't know and you're really listening intently, people want to help you, they want to share."

10. Buckingham and Goodall, *Nine Lies about Work*.

11. Figure 4, "Pendleton's rules of feedback", from *The Consultation: An Approach to Learning and Teaching* by David Pendleton (Oxford University Press). Copyright © David Pendleton 1984. Reprinted by permission of David Pendleton.

12. Neurodiversity refers to diversity in the human brain and in cognition – for example, in sociability, learning, attention, mood and other mental functions. The term was coined in 1998 by sociologist Judy Singer. Thinking about attention deficit hyperactivity disorder, the following study looks at creativity: H. A. White and P. Shah, "Creative style and achievement in adults with

attention-deficit/hyperactivity disorder", *Personality and Individual Differences*, 50(5) (2011).

13. See Chapter 9 for ideas.

14. As an example of a wellness action plan, see Mind's "Guide for employees: wellness action plans (WAPs)", mind-guide-for-employees-wellness-action-plans_final.pdf

Part 3: How to give good feedback

1. Found poems take existing texts and refashion them, reorder them and present them as poems. The literary equivalent of a collage, found poetry is often made from newspaper articles, street signs, graffiti, speeches, letters or even other poems. A pure found poem consists exclusively of outside texts: the words of the poem remain as they were found, with few additions or omissions. Decisions of form, such as where to break a line, are left to the poet.

Chapter 7: Preparation: being clear

1. The PACES model was inspired by the 1981 film, *Chariots of Fire*.

   Harold Abrahams, a runner, has just lost a race. He is despairing and looking for help; he wants to win. His new coach, Sam, says he can help him improve his time. "I can find you thirty seconds, Mr Abrahams," he says. How does he do that?

   He doesn't say, "Just run faster, Harold." That wouldn't be helpful, would it? If Harold could run faster, that's what he would do anyway.

   What the coach does is run Harold through some films of his performance and compare them with films of other runners. This shows Harold some of the techniques (or behaviours) he could learn to use at different points in the race to improve his performance.

   So if you are going to provide clear, properly interrogated feedback, you have to put your feedback data through its PACES in the same way as Sam and Harold. "Film" the behaviours and use them for discussion.

Chapter 8: Anticipation: being helpful

1. Ideas developed drawing on training sessions by esb-training.co.uk

2. Stone and Heen, *Thanks For the Feedback*.

Chapter 9: Implementation: being human
1. Chartered Management Institute (CMI), "Handling difficult conversations", CMI resources.
2. E. Kübler-Ross, *On Death and Dying* (London: Routledge, 1969). Psychiatrist Elisabeth Kübler-Ross initially produced this model as a way of understanding the emotions associated with bereavement. Her model depicts five stages of grief: denial, anger, bargaining, depression and acceptance.
3. Neurodiversity refers to diversity in the human brain and in cognition for example in sociability, learning, attention, mood and other mental functions.
4. For example, the Pomodoro technique is a popular time-management method invented by the Italian Francesco Cirillo. He wrote: "I discovered that you could learn how to improve your effectiveness and be better able to estimate how long a task will take to complete by recording how you utilize your time."

    1. The technique is popular, perhaps because it's portable and easy to learn.
    2. Pick one project or task you want to focus on.
    3. Set a timer for 25–30 minutes, and get to work.
    4. When the buzzer sounds, take a break of two or three minutes.
    5. Repeat.
    6. After four sessions, take a longer break.
    7. Record each session with a tick or X in your notebook.

    The Pomodoro technique is useful if you get distracted while working on a project or want to understand how long a task takes. It's ideal for many types of work including writing, coding, design and study. The technique also works if you have a lot of repetitive work to get through, such as wading through a busy inbox.

Index

References to diagrams, checklists and tables are shown in *italics*

preferred means of 53
Ray Dalio 53
skills in 14, 17–18, 29, 53,
  60–61
speakers 23
styles of 88–94, 120–21
two models 23
very basis of feedback *see*
  feedback: communication
  the very basis of
compassionate candour 43,
  44, 119
competencies
  appraisal system based on
    95–6
  Buckingham and Goodall on
    218 n4, 219 n6
  competency models 218 n4
  Dalio's methods 39
  frameworks 20, 21
  overestimating 220 n7
  raters' personalities 107
compliance 123
concepts
  feedback as 40
  intellectual concepts
    120–21
  reflection giving rise to 17,
    19, 62–3
conceptual thinking 106
conditioning 101

confirmation bias 41, 102–3,
  109
conversations 180–86,
  189–97
  active listening *168*
  anticipating 158, 164–5
  coaching 176
  diagram *160*
  difficult conversations 189–
    97, 208–9
  FORCES: regular 213
  interpreting 129
  purpose of 161–2
  reason for 172
  six golden rules 213–14
  types of 82–3
  unhelpful ones 173
courses 23, 53, 99, 107
Crisp, Quentin 73, 222 n1
  (Chapter 4)

D
Dalio, Ray
  communication style 53
  direct feedback approach
    37, 42
  feedback from junior staff
    47
  Kim Scott and 44
  online outcomes from
    methods 64